DWIGHT D. EISENHOWER
1890-1969

Chronology-Documents-Bibliographical Aids

Edited by

ROBERT I. VEXLER

Series Editor

HOWARD F. BREMER

1970

OCEANA PUBLICATIONS, INC.

Dobbs Ferry, New York

Library of Congress Catalog Card Number: 71-95014
Standard Book Number 379-12070-4

Manufactured in the United States of America

CONTENTS

BIBLIOGRAPHICAL AIDS

EDITOR'S FOREWORD

Every attempt has been made to cite the most accurate dates in this Chronology. Diaries, documents, letters, and similar evidence have been used to determine the exact date. If, however, later scholarship has found such dates to be obviously erroneous, the more plausible date has been used. Should this Chronology be in conflict with other authorities, the student is urged to go back to original sources as well as to such careful biographers as Arthur Stanley Link.

This is a research tool compiled primarily for the student. While it does make some judgments on the significance of the events, it is hoped that they are reasoned judgments based on a long acquaintance with American History.

Obviously, the very selection of events by any writer is itself a judgment.

The essence of these little books is in their making available some pertinent facts and key documents *plus* a critical bibliography which should direct the student to investigate for himself additional and/or contradictory material. The works cited may not always be available in small libraries, but neither are they usually the old, out of print, type of book often included in similar accounts.

CHRONOLOGY

EARLY LIFE AND CAREER

1890

October 14   Born at Denison, Texas. Father David Jacob. Mother Ida Elizabeth Stoever.

1892

Eisenhower family returned to Abilene, Kansas.

June 17   Brother Roy Jacob Eisenhower born.

1894

May 13   Brother Paul A. Eisenhower born. Died March 16, 1895.

1898

February 1   Brother Earl Dewey Eisenhower born.

1899

September 15   Brother Milton Stoever Eisenhower born.

1909

June   Graduated from Abilene High School, Abilene, Kansas. Worked at local creamery.

1910

Took Naval Academy entrance examination with West Point as optional choice. Since he was past his 20th birthday and too old for Annapolis, Eisenhower entered West Point.

1911

June 14   Entered United States Military Academy, West Point, New York. Eisenhower played football until he was forced out by a broken leg. He then became a cheerleader.

1914

August   Outbreak of World War I.

1915

June 12 Graduated from United States Military Academy (61st in class of 164, 95th in deportment). Eisenhower was commissioned a second lieutenant in the infantry and was assigned to the 19th infantry at San Antonio, Texas (served at Fort Sam Houston from September 13, 1915 to May 28, 1917).

October Met Mamie Geneva Doud.

1916

July 1 Married Mary (Mamie) Geneva Doud in Denver, Colorado.

1917

April 6 United States declared war on Germany.

May 15 Promoted to rank of captain.

May 29 Went to Leon Springs, Texas, as regimental supply officer. Served until September 18.

September 19 Went to Fort Ogelthorpe, Georgia, serving as instructor at Officers Training Camp until February 28, 1918.

September 24 Son David Dwight Eisenhower born at Fort Meade, Maryland.

1918

March 25 Commanded 6,000 men at Tank Training Center, Camp Colt, near Gettysburg, Pennsylvania. Served at Army training post in World War I, but did not go overseas. Served at Center until November 18.

November 11 Armistice signed at 5 A.M. in Europe, bringing the cessation of hostilities at 11 A.M.

November 19 Assigned temporary rank of lieutenant colonel in Tank Corps. Served at Camp Dix, New Jersey, until December 22.

December 23 Served at Fort Benning, Georgia, until March 15, 1919.

1920

July 2 Promoted to permanent rank of major.

1921

January 2 Son, David Dwight Eisenhower, died of scarlet fever at Camp Meade, Maryland.

1922

Served as Executive Officer at Camp Gaillard, Panama Canal Zone, from 1922 to September 19, 1924.

1923

August 3 Son, John Sheldon Doud Eisenhower born at Denver, Colorado.

1924

September Served as Recruiting Officer at Fort Logan, Colorado, until August 19, 1925.

1925-1926

Attended Command and General Staff School, Fort Leavenworth, Kansas. Graduated first in a class of 275.

1926

August 15 Joined 24th Infantry at Fort Benning, Georgia.

1927

January 15 Transferred to Washington for service with the American Battle Monuments Commission.

1928

Attended Army War College, Washington, D.C.

1929

Served as Assistant Executive in the Office of the Assistant Secretary of War until February 20, 1933. During this period Eisenhower drafted a plan for wartime industrial mobilization and raw materials supply.

1933

February 21 Served in the Chief of Staff's Office in Washington until September 24, 1935.

Attended Army Industrial College:

1935

Major in the United States Army. Served as assistant to General Douglas MacArthur in the Philippines, 1933-1939.

1936

July 1 Promoted to permanent rank of lieutenant colonel.

1937

May 19   After taking flight lessons, Eisenhower made his first solo flight.

1939

September 1   World War II began. Germany invaded Poland. Great Britain and France declared war on Germany.

November 30   Received pilot's license, number 93,258.

1940

February   Returned to the United States from the Philippines; joined the 15th Infantry in Ord, California. Regiment then moved to Fort Lewis, Washington.

1941

March 11   Appointed Chief of Staff of the Third Army, with the temporary rank of brigadier general, at San Antonio, Texas.

December 7   Japanese attacked United States Naval Base at Pearl Harbor, Hawaii.

December 8   United States declared war on Japan.

December 11   Germany and Italy declared war on the United States, which then recognized the existence of a state of war with these nations.

December 14   General George C. Marshall called Eisenhower to Washington.

1942

February 19   Appointed Chief of the War Plans Division of the War Department General Staff.

March 10   Father David Jacob Eisenhower died in Abilene, Kansas.

April   Appointed Assistant Chief of Staff in charge of the Operations Division of the War Department General Staff with the temporary rank of major general.

June 25   Appointed Commanding General, European Theatre of Operations.

July 7   Assigned temporary rank of lieutenant general. Went to London for strategy discussions with the British.

November 7   Appointed Commander-in-chief of Allied forces in North Africa. Issued proclamation to the French in North Africa asking for their cooperation, indicating signals to be used to help prevent unnecessary bloodshed.

November 13   Appealed to the French Fleet at Toulon to join the United Nations against Hitler by sailing to Gibraltar.

November 28   Met with Air Chiefs of the United States and Great Britain at his headquarters in North Africa.

1943

February 6   Appointed Commander of United States North African Theatre of Operations.

February 7-8   Conferred with Prime Minister Winston Churchill, of Great Britain.

February 11   Promoted to temporary rank of full general.

May 26   General Eisenhower and General Douglas MacArthur were appointed Honorary Knights, Grand Cross of the Most Honorable Order of the Bath, by King George VI.

July 9   Directed invasions of Sicily by United States, British and Canadian troops.

July 29   In a message to the Italian people broadcast from Algiers, General Eisenhower offered immediate peace.

September 8   Announced the unconditional surrender of Italy from his North African headquarters.

August 31   Promoted to permanent rank of major general.

October 30   The *Army and Navy Journal* correctly predicted that General Eisenhower would become United States Army Chief of Staff if General George C. Marshall were appointed Supreme Commander of Anglo-American forces.

December 24 Appointed Supreme Commander, Allied Expeditionary Force.

1944

January 16 Arrived in London to take command of Allied invasion forces after talks with Prime Minister Winston Churchill in Marakesh, Morocco, and with President Franklin Delano Roosevelt and General George C. Marshall in Washington, D.C.

February 18 Awarded the Order of Suvarov, first class, highest Russian military decoration.

June 6 Led D-Day invasion of Normandy.

August Moved his Supreme Command Headquarters to Normandy.

September 15 Formally took command of the United States Seventh Army.

September 28 Issued proclamation to Germany saying that the Allies are coming "as conquerors not as oppressors" to eradicate the Nazi Party and militarism from Germany.

December 15 Senate voted new 5-star rank to Generals Dwight D. Eisenhower, Douglas MacArthur, George C. Marshall, and Henry H. Arnold and to Admirals William D. Leahy, Ernest J. King, and Chester W. Nimitz.

December 29 General Eisenhower and Herbert H. Lehman, Director General of the United Nations Relief and Rehabilitation Administration signed formal agreement fixing the responsibilities of UNRRA for assisting allied military authorities in Western Europe during their period of responsibility for relief.

1945

April 12 President Franklin Delano Roosevelt died at Warm Springs, Georgia, of a cerebral hemorrhage. Harry S Truman sworn in as President of the United States.

April 24   General Eisenhower asked the United Nations War Crimes Commission to send investigators to German concentration camps to make an official survey of conditions. 12 members left by air on April 26.

May 7   Accepted surrender of German Army at Rheims, France, at his school house headquarters at 2:41 A.M. French time (V. E. Day).

May-
November   Commander of United States occupation forces in Europe.

June 2   Urged peacetime draft in a letter to the House of Representatives.

June 10   Received Russia's highest award, the jeweled order of victory from Marshal Gregory K. Zhukov in Frankfort, Germany.

June 18   Returned to the United States. In Washington, General Eisenhower was given the greatest reception ever accorded a hero. In an address to the Congress he stressed the need for the unity of the Allies in peace as in war.

June 22   In Abilene, Kansas, General Eisenhower told reporters that he had no political ambitions.

July 10   Returned to his headquarters at Frankfurt-on-the-Main, Germany.

September 6   Received Belgium's highest decoration at official ceremonies during a visit to Brussels.

September 13   Conferred with Pope Pius XII, culminating a 2-day sightseeing tour of Italy.

September 25   Issued new order prohibiting any firm from employing members of the Nazi Party in any capacity but common labor on threat of being closed. General George S. Patton, Jr., who disagreed with the importance of denazification, was relieved of his post as military governor of Bavaria.

November 19   Served as Chief of Staff of the United States Army until February 7, 1947.

1946

January 9	Ordered overseas commanders to send home all men for whom there was no military need in order of highest score and longest service.
January 31	Received honorary Doctor of Laws degree from Boston University.
March 28	Appointed member of 10-man military "brain trust" by President Harry S Truman in order to plan national defense.
April 2	Received Freedom House Award for 1945.
April 17	Awarded Norway's highest military honor, the Order of St. Olaf, Degree of Grand Commander by Ambassador Morgenstierne in Washington, D.C.
April 26	Set up an 18-month training and organization plan emphasizing air power, scientific research and world-wide intelligence service.
April 29	Began inspection tour of the Pacific.
June 9	Delivered commencement address at Norwich University, Northfield, Vermont, indicating limitations to unilateral disarmament and urging support of the United Nations.
June 14	Received the 1945 American Hebrew Medal for promoting better understanding between Christians and Jews.
June 28	*Eisenhower's Own Story of the War* published.
August 6	Received the Brazilian Government's order of Merit in Rio de Janeiro.
September 11	Mother Ida Elizabeth Stoever Eisenhower died in Abilene, Kansas.
October 13	Awarded the Theodore Roosevelt Distinguished Service Medal for 1946 along with Irving Berlin, General Douglas MacArthur and Admirals William F. Halsey, Jr. and Chester W. Nimitz.

1947

February 21 Awarded honorary Doctor of Laws degree by Columbia University.

February 25 Opened the United Jewish Appeal's Drive in Washington for $170 million for the relief of European Jewry.

May 27 Addressed the National Board of Fire Underwriters in New York, urging a national war-prevention drive.

June 10 Son, John Sheldon Doud Eisenhower married to Barbara Jean Thompson in Fort Monroe, Virginia.

June 17 Awarded honorary LLD Degree from Princeton University along with President Harry S Truman and others.

June 24 Accepted post of Presidency of Columbia University effective when he retired as Army Chief of Staff early in 1948.

August 29 Addressed American Legion Convention.

September 11 Announced in New York that he would not be a party to draft him for the Presidency.

October 20 Awarded Denmark's highest decoration, the Knight of the Elephant.

December 12 Lieutenant Colonel J. H. Michaelis, General Eisenhower's military aid, said in letter to the National Council for Prevention of War, that General Eisenhower asked him to say that he was not a candidate for political office.

1948

January 23 Withdrew from the Presidential race after being entered in several Presidential primaries.

February 7 Retired from active duty in the Army, but retained 5-star rank.

March 31 Grandson, David Eisenhower 2nd, born at West Point, New York, to Captain and Mrs. John Eisenhower.

May 2	Retired from the army.
June 7	Formally appointed President of Columbia University.
July 5	After much pressure to accept the Presidential nomination, General Eisenhower reiterated his refusal to run as a candidate of either party. Telegram of July 9 ended once and for all the draft campaign.
October 12	Formally installed as thirteenth President of Columbia University.
November 22	Published *Crusade in Europe.*

1949

February 11	Appointed temporary presiding officer of the Joint Chiefs of Staff by President Truman.
March 21	Addressed Mayors Conference in Washington, urging them not to expect the federal government to solve all local problems.
September 5	Addressed opening session of American Bar Association in St. Louis, stressing a middle-of-the-road course for America.
November 21	Presided over first annual Freedoms Foundation Awards.
November 22	Told reporters in Cincinnati, Ohio, that he was not seeking any political office.

1950

June 25	North Korean Communist forces equipped with Soviet-made weapons invaded South Korea.
July 4	Delivered address at Boy Scout Jamboree at Valley Forge, Pennsylvania, stating that he supported as inescapable, the United States' decision to aid Korea.
September 4	Opened the privately-sponsored Crusade for Freedom in Denver, Colorado; a campaign to broadcast the truth about democracy to people behind the Iron Curtain.

December 16 Granted indefinite leave of absence from Columbia University to serve as Commander of NATO forces in Europe. Officially appointed to post on December 19.

1951

January 12-18 Toured North Atlantic Pact capitals.

January 20-23 Paid goodwill visit to Germany as Atlantic Pact Supreme Commander.

February 2 Delivered nation wide radio-television address urging support for NATO.

February 22 Awarded Freedoms Foundation Prize for his speech, "Only an Informed Public Opinion Can Win the Peace."

May 8-10 Visited Belgium and the Netherlands.

May 16 Designated Oslo, Norway, and Fontanebleau, France, as sites for subordinate northern and southern Command Headquarters of the Allied Powers in Europe.

May 21-24 Visited Norway and Denmark.

August 27 Eisenhower's name was entered provisionally as a Democratic candidate for President in Oregon's May, 1952 primary election, where a candidate's consent is not needed.

1952

January Eisenhower's name entered in first Republican Presidential primary.

March 11 Won New Hampshire primary, getting all 14 Republican delegates.

March 30 President Harry S. Truman announced that he would not be a candidate for reelection to the Presidency.

April 15 Won New Jersey primary, winning at least 31 of 38 delegates.

April 29 Won Massachusetts primary, winning 29 of 38 convention delegates.

April 30   Visited Frankfurt-on-the-Main, Germany, for a farewell review of United States troops in Germany.

May 5-6   Visited Rome, Italy.

May 30   Turned over command of Allied forces in Europe to General Matthew B. Ridgway.

June 2   Retired from the Army in order to campaign for the Republican Presidential nomination.

July 7-12   Republic National Convention at Chicago, Illinois, nominated Dwight David Eisenhower for President and Senator Richard Milhous Nixon of California for Vice President.

                  The Eisenhower group had brought the dispute with the Taft supporters over credentials of delegates from four southern states on to the floor of the Convention. Eisenhower delegates from Georgia and Texas were seated.

July 18   Resigned as General of the Army.

July 21-26   Democratic National Convention at Chicago, Illinois, nominated Governor Adlai Ewing Stevenson of Illinois for President and Senator John Jackson Sparkman of Alabama for Vice President.

August 25   Eisenhower told the American Legion Convention that the United States should help the people of Communist countries to "liberate" themselves. This statement created quite a furor.

September 10 Delivered address in Philadelphia, Pennsylvania, outlining his own 10-point program to win peace and prevent future Koreas.

September 12 Senator Robert Taft of Ohio presented Eisenhower with a statement of doctrines which Eisenhower was to approve as the price of old-line Republicans' support.

September 23 Republican Vice Presidential nominee Richard M. Nixon made a television address to the nation answering attacks made upon him that he had a second salary paid from a "secret millionaires' fund." Public opinion turned in favor of him as result of the address.

October 24 General Eisenhower announced that if he were elected President he would visit Korea in order to study the situation first hand.

November 4 National Elections. Dwight David Eisenhower elected President. Eisenhower received 33,778,963 votes winning 442 electoral votes and Adlai Stevenson received 27,314,992 votes winning 89 electoral votes.

November 17 Resigned from Columbia University effective January 19, 1953.

November 18 Held conference at the White House with President Harry S Truman to begin work on exchange of information.

December 2-5 As President-Elect, Eisenhower visited Korea carrying out his campaign pledge.

1953

January 7 Senator John W. Bricker of Ohio proposed an amendment to the Constitution to limit the scope of international treaties to which the United States could be a party to and to impose controls on the power of the President to negotiate treaties and executive agreements. The Senate rejected the amendment on February 26, 1953, by 60-31, 1 vote short of the 2/3 required majority. Eisenhower and John Foster Dulles, Secretary of State-designate, opposed the amendment.

FIRST TERM IN OFFICE

January 20 Inaugurated as 34th President. Oath administered by Chief Justice Frederick Moore Vinson.

January 21 Cabinet Appointments: Secretary of State John Foster Dulles of Washington, D.C., Secretary of the Treasury George Magoffin Humphrey of Ohio, Attorney General Herbert Brownell, Jr. of New York, Postmaster General

Arthur Ellsworth Summerfield of Michigan, Secretary of the Interior Douglas McKay of Oregon, Secretary of Agriculture Ezra Taft Benson of Utah, Secretary of Commerce Sinclair Weeks of Massachusetts, and Secretary of Labor Martin Patrick Durkin of Illinois.

January 26   Created a 9-man board headed by William H. Jackson to study the problem of unifying United States psychological warfare.

January 28   Appointed Charles Erwin Wilson of Michigan, Secretary of Defense.

February 1   Received into membership of National Presbyterian Church of Washington, D.C.

February 2   Announced ending of neutralization of Formosa by Seventh Fleet.

February 3   All controls on wages and salaries, as well as many consumer goods lifted.

February 7   Senator William F. Knowland of California called for a United States naval blockade of Red China. Eisenhower opposed this plan as a virtual act of war.

February 11   Refused to grant executive clemency to Ethel and Julius Rosenberg, convicted atomic spies, who were under death sentences.

February 20   "Captive Peoples" Resolution introduced into both Houses of Congress deploring "the forcible absorption of free peoples into an aggressive despotism" and denouncing Soviet attempts at subjugation of free peoples. Resolution shelved March 7 after announcement of Marshal Josef Stalin's death.

February 25   Announced at press conferenc het he would go to any reasonable place to meet Premier Stalin if he, Eisenhower, thought that it would be of value to world peace.

March 5   Death of Stalin announced in Moscow.

March 10   Signed bill increasing by $500 million the authority of the Federal Housing Administration to insure home maintenance and repair.

March 12   Submitted reorganization plan to Congress designed to convert the Federal Security agency into a new cabinet department of health, education, and welfare.

March 17   Price controls officially ended by Office of Price Stabilization.

April 1   Signed into law a bill creating the new Cabinet post, the Department of Health, Education, and Welfare, effective April 11, 1953. Appointed Oveta Culp Hobby of Texas as first secretary.

April 2   Japan and the United States signed a 10-year treaty of friendship, commerce, and navigation.

April 12   Named his brother, Dr. Milton S. Eisenhower, to be his personal representative on a good will and fact-finding mission to Latin America.

April 16   Delivered major foreign policy address in which he outlined a specific series of peaceful acts which the U.S.S.R. could carry out which would aid in establishing world peace.

April 20   United States Communist Party was ordered to register with the Justice Department as an organization which was controlled and directed by Russia.

April 27   Extended rule of security to all government employees under which employees found untrustworthy for defects of behavior or character such as drunkenness, drug addiction, mental illness or sexual perversion were discharged.

April 30   Signed Rent Control bill extending Federal rent controls through July 31.

May 4-6   Conference of state and territorial governors with the President at Washington, D.C.

May 19   Delivered nationwide address calling for a 6-months extension of the excess profits tax beyond June 30, 1953.

May 22   Signed Tidelands Oil Law giving states title to offshore oil.

May 25   First atomic artillery shell fired at proving grounds in Nevada.

May 28-
September 30 3002 security risks discharged from federal employment.

June 2   Ordered the creation of an international organization employee loyalty board to evaluate as security risks United States citizens employed by or applying for jobs with the United Nations.

June 19   Execution of atomic spies Julius and Ethel Rosenberg, first spies sentenced to death by a United States civil court and the first execution for treason in peacetime.

July 25-27 Attended conference for defense leaders at Quantico, Virginia.

July 27   Korean War ended with the signing of the armistice, calling for a demilitarized zone and voluntary repatriation of prisoners at Panmunjon, Korea.

July 31   Death of Senator Robert A. Taft. William F. Knowland of California became Senate Majority Leader.

August-
September American prisoners of war in Korea repatriated.

August 1   New Foreign Operations Administration given direction of all foreign aid programs.

August 6   Vetoed bill exempting motion picture theatres from the 20% federal admissions tax.

August 7   Signed Refugee Relief Act of 1953 admitting 214,000 refugees beyond the regular immigration quotas.

August 8   Premier Malenkov declared that the U.S.S.R. stood for "peaceful coexistence of the two systems," but demanding acceptance of Red China as a Big Five Power and the banning of "atomic and other arms of mass destruction."

August 12   Soviet Union exploded a hydrogen bomb.

President Eisenhower signed bill authorizing the states of New York and New Jersey to create a bistate waterfront commission to clean up stevedoring operations in New York harbor.

August 13   Created a new four-member committee to prevent racial and religious discriminatory practices by companies with United States contracts.

August 14   Announced appointment of Clarence B. Randall, Chairman of the Board of Inland Steel as Chairman of the new Commission on Foreign Economic Policy.

August 20   Soviet Government announced that it had tested a hydrogen bomb within the past few days—confirmed by the Atomic Energy Commission.

September 7   Chief Justice Frederick Moore Vinson died.

September 10 Secretary of Labor Martin P. Durkin resigned because of the failure of the administration to carry out an alleged agreement to propose several amendments to the Taft-Hartley Labor Law.

September 26 Spain authorized the United States to develop, maintain and use military bases in that country in return for economic and military aid.

October 5   Appointed Earl Warren of California Chief Justice of the Supreme Court.

October 9   Appointed James Paul Mitchell of New Jersey Secretary of Labor.

October 15-20 Made a tour of the Western states.

November 6   Attorney General Herbert Brownell told a luncheon club in Chicago that when President Truman appointed Harry Dexter White to the International Monetary Fund in 1946, he knew that White was a Communist spy. The House Un-American Affairs Committee issued a subpoena to former President Truman who ignored it as a violation of the constitutional separation of powers, but explained his action in a television address.

November 7 William L. Borden; former executive secretary of the Joint Congressional Committee on Atomic Energy, told J. Edgar Hoover, head of the Federal Bureau of Investigation, that J. Robert Oppenheimer was probably a Soviet spy.

November 13- 15 Visited Canada.

December 4-7 Conferred at Bermuda with British Prime Minister Winston Churchill and French Premier Joseph Laniel on the exchange of atomic information.

December 8 Delivered address to the United Nations General Assembly calling upon the U.S.S.R. to join the United States in contributing part of its atomic stockpile to an international pool available for peaceful uses.

December- January 1964 Climax of McCarthy Senate hearings investigating alleged subversion in the Signal Corps Engineering Laboratories at Fort Monmouth, New Jersey.

1954

January 11 Delivered messages to Congress proposing 15 changes in the Taft-Hartley Labor Law and urging a return to flexible price supports.

January 12 Secretary of State John Foster Dulles announced to the nation that this country would henceforth follow a defense policy based on "massive retaliation."

January 14 Proposed in a special message to Congress that larger social security benefits be provided for more workers without disturbing the existing system in principle.

January 18 Proposed to Congress that provision be made for federal reinsurance of private health insurance plans.

January 21 First atomic submarine, *Nautilus,* launched.

January 25-
February 18 Berlin Conference of Foreign Ministers failed to reach an agreement on the reunification of Germany.

January 26 Senate approved ratification of a mutual security treaty between the United States and South Korea.

March 1 Five representatives wounded in House of Representatives by Puerto Rican nationalists.

United States set off second hydrogen bomb explosion at Bikini atoll revealing considerable fallout peril.

March 8 Mutual defense agreement signed by Japan and the United States, providing for gradual rearmament of Japan.

March 13 Vietminh began siege of French forces at Dienbienphu, in French Indochina, which they successfully brought to a conclusion on May 7.

March 24 President Eisenhower announced that Southeast Asia was "of the most transcendent importance to the United States and the Free World." On March 30, Secretary of State Dulles called for united action in Indochina.

March 31 Signed bill providing for an estimated $999,000,000 annual reduction in federal excise taxes.

April 1 Signed into law a measure authorizing the establishment of an Air Force Academy similar to West Point and Annapolis. First class sworn in at Lowry Air Force Base, Denver, Colorado, July 11, 1955.

April 8 United States and Canada announced construction of an early warning radar net stretching across 3000 miles of Canadian far north.

April 12 Beginning of secret hearings concerning alleged Communist hearings of J. Robert Oppenheimer, wartime head of the Los Alamos Laboratory who had been suspended by Executive Order in December of 1953. The Committee cleared Oppenheimer as "loyal" but decided against his reinstatement as an Atomic Energy Commission consultant.

April 16   President Eisenhower stated in a formal declaration that after European Defense Community Treaty came into force the United States would regard any action threatening the community as a threat to the United States.

April 17   Vice President Richard Nixon tested American public opinion by indicating that United States troops might be sent to French Indochina.

April 20   Secretary of State John Foster Dulles left for Europe for conferences with various United States allies, Britain and France, prior to his attendance at the Geneva Peace Conference.

April 22-   Army-McCarthy hearings arising out of Senator Joseph
June 17   McCarthy's charges of subversive activities.

April 26-   Geneva Conference on the Indo-Chinese problems held.
June 15

April 30   State Department announced that Under Secretary of State Walter Bedell Smith would replace Secretary Dulles at the Geneva Conference.

May 4   Secretary of State Dulles left the Geneva Conference. He had become disgruntled over the demand of Chinese Foreign Minister Chou-En-lai and Russian Foreign Minister Molotov that the United States give up all its allies in Asia, stop economic aid to its friends, and the refusal of the Communists to allow free elections in Korea.

May 9   President Eisenhower issued an order establishing an internal security division of the Justice Department to expedite the prosecution of spies and saboteurs.

May 13   Signed St. Lawrence Seaway bill authorizing joint construction by the United States and Canada.

May 17   Supreme Court in *Brown vs. Board of Education of Topeka* (347 U.S. 483) reversed *Plessy vs. Ferguson* (1896) with its "separate but equal doctrine" unanimously declaring that racial segregation in schools was unconstitutional.

May 19-
June 22 5-Power subcommittee of United Nations Disarmament Conference held secret meetings in London. Favored banning of atomic and nuclear weapons but failed to agree on issue of inspection and one-third cut in conventional forces.

May 24 Supreme Court upheld provision of Internal Security Act of 1950, making past membership in the Communist Party a ground for the deportation of aliens.

June 8 Received honorary degree from Washington University.

June 25-29 Conferred with Prime Minister Winston Churchill at Washington, D.C. on world peace.

June 29 President Eisenhower and Prime Minister Churchill issued the Potomac Charter stating that they would not participate in the "unwilling subordination" of former sovereign states into slavery, and that they would continue to work to unite nations which are "divided against their will."

July 2 President Eisenhower signed three educational bills into law providing for state and White House conferences on educational research and a National Advisory Committee on Education.

July 12 Proposed a 4-point program calling for joint modernization of United States highways by federal and state governments at a cost of several billion dollars.

July 16 Approved plan under which Edgar H. Dixon and Eugene A. Yates, electric power executives in the South, agreed to build a $100 million private plant to supply additional electric power not supplied by the Tennessee Valley Authority. Scandal occurred because Adolphe H. Wenzell who advised the Government to carry out this venture was Vice President of the First Boston Corporation which was to finance the construction.

July 21 Geneva agreement signed to end war in Indochina after French withdrawal. The United States and the Vietnamese refused to sign the treaty, but Under Secretary of State Walter Bedell Smith indicated that the United States would not disrupt the arrangement.

August 2   Signed Housing Act of 1954 to build 35,000 houses to serve families displaced by various urban redevelopment programs.

August 5   United States mediated the British-Iranian oil dispute. An 8-firm consortium was to produce and market the oil with a 50-50 split of payment with Iran.

August 7   United States government issued white paper designed to alert all governments of the western hemisphere to the danger of international Communism.

August 10   Signed Securities Information bill permitting greater distribution of information on new investment security issues during waiting period between filing of statement with the Securities Exchange Commission and effective date.

August 16   Signed Internal Revenue Code of 1964, completely revising Internal Revenue Laws and making important substantive and procedural modifications.

August 23   Vetoed bill providing for 5% increase in the salaries of federal employees.

August 24   Signed Communist Control Act outlawing Communist Party, but party membership not made a crime.

August 28   Signed Farm bill providing for flexible price supports.

August 30   Signed Atomic Energy Act imposing stringent restrictions on transfer of nuclear materials outside the jurisdiction of the United States.

September 1   Signed Social Security Act extending Social Security coverage to 10 million additional persons including farmers and professional people.

September 3   Signed Espionage and Sabotage Act of 1954 authorizing death penalty for peacetime espionage and sabotage.

September 6   World atomic pool established without Soviet Union because of failure to reach agreement with the U.S.S.R. on "atoms for peace" program.

September 8   Southeast Asia Defense Treaty signed in Manila by delegates of 8 nations: Australia, Great Britain, France, New Zealand, Pakistan, the Philippines, Thailand, and the United States. Created the Southeast Asia Treaty Organization (SEATO).

September 30   First atomic powered submarine U.S.S. *Nautilus* commissioned at Groton, Connecticut.

October 3   London Conference of Foreign Ministers admitted West Germany to NATO.

October 8   President Eisenhower called for election of a Republican Congress to avoid the cold war of partisan politics.

October 23   Stated in a letter to South Vietnamese Premier Ngo Dinh Diem that the United States expected Vietnam to effect needed reforms.

October 25   First telecast of a Cabinet meeting to hear Secretary of State John Foster Dulles report on the agreements made at Paris in regard to Germany.

October 28   Made an impassioned appeal in Denver, Colorado, during the electional campaign saying that if the Democrats won majorities in Congress a "cold war of partisan politics" between the Executive and Legislative branches would result.

November 2   National elections. Democrats narrowly regained control of Congress.

November 3   President Eisenhower announced initation of new phase of negotiations with U.S.S.R. on atomic energy.

December 2   Senate voted condemnation of Senator Joseph R. McCarthy for conduct during Senate hearings, based on the recommendations of a Select Committee chaired by Senator Arthur V. Watkins of Utah. This Committee has been appointed as a result of the movement for censure led by Senator Ralph E. Flanders of Vermont.

United States and Nationalist China signed a mutual defense pact promising United States action if the Communists attacked Nationalist Chinese territory.

December 7   Senator Joseph R. McCarthy made a bitter personal attack on President Eisenhower for alleged weakness in dealing with Communists.

December 11   President Eisenhower created a Council of Foreign Economic Policy headed by Joseph M. Dodge to coordinate foreign aid activities and develop other United States foreign economic policies.

December 28   Secretary of State John Foster Dulles indicated at press conference that aggression in western Europe would be met with tactical atomic weapons.

1955

January 1   United States Foreign Operations Administration began to supply direct financial aid to South Vietnam, Cambodia, and Laos.

January 10   President Eisenhower delivered a special message to Congress asking for new powers to reduce foreign trade barriers including a three-year extension of Reciprocal Trade Agreements Act.

January 13   Asked Congress to inaugurate a military reserve plan, extend the Selective Service System and to raise military pay, allowances, and benefits.

January 19   First Presidential news conference to be recorded by both news reels and television.

January 24   Asked Congress for a free hand in the use of United States forces to defend Formosa against Communist aggression. Request was approved January 28.

January 25   United States and Panama signed a treaty of cooperation concerning the Panama Canal.

January 31   Submitted a proposal for a national health program to Congress.

February 6   Urged state governors in a letter to have all states enact laws to give servicemen overseas effective opportunities to vote.

February 7   United States Seventh Fleet helped evacuation of Communist threatened Tachen Islands near Formosa.

February 8   Proposed 3-year $7 billion emergency federal-state-local school construction program to Congress.

February 22   Submitted a 10-year federal-state-local highway construction program to Congress at a total cost of $101 billion.

February 23   Stated that the United States would stop testing atomic weapons only under a workable disarmament agreement with effective international inspection.

March 2   Signed Congressional-Judicial pay bill granting federal employees the highest salaries ever paid to government officials.

March 16   State Department released secret Yalta Conference papers.

President Eisenhower indicated at press conference that the United States would use tactical atomic weapons in case of war.

March 19   Named Foreign Operations Administrator Harold E. Stassen to newly created post of Special assistant on disarmament problems with cabinet rank.

March 28   Appointed John Marshall Harlan of New York Associate Justice of the Supreme Court.

White House announced designation of Rear Admiral Richard E. Byrd to lead a United States expedition to the Antarctic in connection with the International Geophysical Year (1957-58).

March 31   Signed bill providing for increase of $745 million a year in military pay and allowance.

April 1   Senate consented to the ratification of the 1954 agreements setting up an armed sovereign Germany within NATO.

April 9   Established Civil Defense Coordinating Board to be headed by Civil Defense Administrator Val Peterson.

April 12   Jonas E. Salk's antipoliomyelitis vaccine declared "safe, effective and potent" against paralytic polio.

April 16   President Eisenhower ordered the establishment of a semiautonomous International Cooperation Administration within the State Department to adminster long-range foreign economic aid program. Named John B. Hollister of Ohio to head the office on April 30.

April 21   United States occupation of Germany ended; troops remained on a contractual basis.

April 25   Announced plans for an atomic-powered merchant ship to tour the world in the interest of peace.

May 10   The United States, Great Britain, and France sent identical notes to the U.S.S.R. proposing a conference of heads of state accompanied by their foreign ministers.

May 15   Big Four foreign ministers signed treaty restoring sovereignty to Austria.

May 19   President Eisenhower vetoed a bill providing for an average of 8.8% increase in salary for postal workers, claiming it was unfair and too expensive.

May 31   Supreme Court reaffirmed principle of school integration, ordering gradual compliance by local authorities.

June 1   Signed bill making it a crime to threaten a President-elect or Vice President-elect.

June 3   Signed into law an act allowing the Government to give its surplus property to schools and hospitals.

June 10   Signed compromise bill giving an average salary increase of 8% to postal workers.

June 15-17   3-day hydrogen bomb alert testing United States civil defenses.

June 20   In an address at the conference in San Francisco commemorating the tenth anniversary of the United Nations,

President Eisenhower asked for a new kind of peace using the atom for productive purposes.

June 21   Signed bill extending for 3 years the reciprocal trade program.

June 24   Signed Austrian peace treaty reestablishing Austria with her January 1, 1938 frontiers. The Big Four undertook to respect Austria's independence and territorial integrity.

June 23   Signed Act giving more than one million federal employees average pay increases of 7.5%.

June 30   Signed bill authorizing increase of $6 billion in the public debt.

July 1   Signed bill authorizing $75 million to speed completion of Inter-American Highway in three years.

Signed bill requiring inscription "In God We Trust" on all United States currency.

July 11   Announced cancellation of Dixon-Yates private power contract.

July 18-23   Geneva Summit Conference of Big Four Heads of State: President Eisenhower, Premier Bulganin of Russia, Prime Minister Winston Churchill of Great Britain, and Premier Edgar Faure of France.

July 29   White House announced plan to launch small unmanned earth-circling satellites as part of United States participation in the International Geophysical Year.

August 1   United States and Chinese Governments opened talks in Geneva.

President Eisenhower appointed Marion Bayard Folsom of Georgia, Secretary of Health, Education and Welfare.

August 3   Signed bill for four-year $252 million program of federal aid for airport construction.

August 6   Signed Presidential Inaugural Ceremonies Act empowering the inaugural committee to make arrangements and plans for the inauguration.

August 8-20   First conference on peaceful uses of Atomic Energy at Geneva, Switzerland. 73 nations were represented.

August 9   Signed bill creating bi-partisan, 12-member commission to review the Government's employee loyalty-security program.

Dr. Jonas E. Salk awarded $2,500 gold medal for developing polio vaccine.

August 12   Signed bill increasing the Federal minimum wage from 75 cents to $1.00 per hour.

September 24   Suffered heart attack at Denver, Colorado. Hospitalized for two months.

October 12   State Department made public a letter from President Eisenhower to Premier Bulganin offering conditional acceptance of the Soviet plan for reciprocal arms inspection.

October 20   The United States, Soviet Russia and 68 other nations signed the UN Statute of the International Atomic Energy Agency.

November 15   Stated that the United States would do all it could to gain a peaceful settlement between Israel and the Arab states.

November 21-22 Meeting of Baghdad Pact Council: Turkey, Pakistan, Iran, Iraq, and the United Kingdom. On November 29, President Eisenhower issued a declaration of United States support for the pact and for the independence and integrity of its members.

November 22   Presided over first meeting of the Cabinet and the National Security Council since his heart attack.

November 25   Interstate Commerce Commission banned racial segregation on interstate trains and buses.

December 1   Rev. Dr. Martin Luther King led the Montgomery bus boycott which eventually led to the beginning of unsegregated bus service on December 21.

United States, Great Britain, and France rejected a Soviet contention that four-power rule of Berlin had terminated.

December 5   American Federation of Labor (AFL) and Congress of Industrial Organizations (CIO) merged.

December 28   President Eisenhower flew from Washington, D.C. to Key West, Florida, for a rest prescribed by his doctors.

1956

January 6   Delivered special message to Congress urging creation of $1 billion soil bank plan to compensate farmers for reducing crop production and improving soil tilling.

January 10   United States International Cooperation Administration announced allotment of $50 million to India for economic development.

January 12   Asked Congress to approve 5-year, $2 billion program for aid for public school construction.

January 13   Named a board of 8 citizens to monitor activities of Central Intelligence Agency and other units gathering security information.

January 26   Requested Congress to authorize 5-year, $250 million program to expand construction of medical research and teaching facilities.

January 30-
February 1   Conferred with Prime Minister Anthony Eden of Great Britain at Washington, D.C. A communique at the end of the conference warned Asian and African countries against looking to the U.S.S.R. for economic and political aid.

February 8   Called for sweeping changes in United States immigration laws in special message to Congress.

February 14 President Eisenhower's personal physician, Dr. Paul Dudley White, reported after a physical examination that there was no barrier to his seeking and serving a second term.

February 16 Ordered revision of Selective Service regulations virtually exempting fathers and men over 26.

February 17 Vetoed Natural Gas Bill which would have exempted independent producers of natural gas from federal utility rate control after Senator Francis Case of North Dakota revealed that he had been offered a $2,500 campaign contribution by the gas interests.

February 19 Offered to give part of United States farm surplus to relieve suffering in Europe caused by most severe winter in years.

February 20 Signed bill giving permanent federal status to the United States Merchant Marine Academy at Kings Point, New York.

February 29 Announced his availability for a second term.

March 7 Called for immediate action by United Nations to pacify the Middle East.

March 11 Manifesto issued by southern Senators and Representatives pledging use of all legal means to reverse Supreme Court integration ruling.

March 26 President Eisenhower met at White Sulphur Springs, West Virginia, with Canadian Prime Minister St. Laurent and Mexican President Adolfo Ruiz Cortines.

April 3 Created a Federal Council on Aging to coordinate aid to older people.

April 10 In a letter to Congressional leaders, President Eisenhower urged higher pay and better living conditions to stop heavy turnover of trained military personnel.

April 11 Signed bill authorizing $760 million flood control and reclamation project on the upper Colorado River.

April 18	State Department announced agreement among 12 nations, including U.S.S.R., on a charter for the International Atomic Energy Agency.
April 26	Vice President Richard M. Nixon formally notified President Eisenhower that he would accept renomination.
May 4	Atomic Energy Commission authorized private atomic energy plants.
May 9	Signed bill to curb expansion of bank holding companies.
May 28	Signed Soil Bank bill establishing an acreage reserve or "soil bank" Program in order to compensate farmers for reducing their 1956-1959 crops of basic commodities below their allotments.
June 1	Formed a special Cabinet-level committee to work on legislative and administrative means of aiding small business.
June 4	State Department released text of speech by Soviet Communist Party first secretary Nikita Khrushchev attacking Joseph Stalin at the 20th Party Congress in February, 1956.
June 8	Appointed Frederick Andrew Seaton of Nebraska Secretary of the Interior.
June 9	Underwent emergency ileitis operation.
June 13	Signed proclamation giving effect to tariff reductions negotiated by the United States at the 1956 meetings of the General Agreement on Tariffs and Trade at Geneva, Switzerland.
June 19	Signed bill authorizing five-year $7.5 million per year program to develop public library service in rural areas.
June 29	Signed Federal Aid Highway Act providing $32.5 billion over the next 13 years for construction of 41,000 miles of interstate system of highways.
July 3	Signed bill creating a continuing national health survey under which the Public Health Service would interview one family in every 1,000 annually.

July 14   Signed bill authorizing death penalty for anyone causing loss of life by damage to airplane, bus, or any vehicle used to carry passengers in interstate or foreign commerce.

July 18   Signed bill authorizing death penalty for those convicted of selling heroin to persons under 18 years of age.

July 19   United States withdrew offers to finance construction of Aswan Dam in Egypt, precipitating Egyptian seizure of Suez Canal.

July 22   Signed Panama Declaration, affirming principles of the Organization of American States, along with 18 other heads of state.

July 26   Signed bill increasing salaries of cabinet members and other high-ranking federal employees.

July 30   Signed three-year $90 million program of Government grants to help build public and nonprofit health research facilities.

August 1   Signed Social Security amendments establishing a system of disability insurance and making women eligible for social security benefits at 62 instead of 65.

Signed bill incorporating the National Music Council.

August 3   Signed bill creating an office of Federal Highway Administrator to carry out $33 billion federal highway construction program.

August 6   Signed bill permitting the Federal Bureau of Investigation to begin investigation of kidnapping cases after expiration of 24 hours instead of seven days.

August 13-17   Democratic National Convention at Chicago, Illinois, nominated Adlai Ewing Stevenson of Illinois for President and Estes Kefauver of Tennessee for Vice President.

August 20-24   Republican National Convention at San Francisco, California, renominated President Dwight David Eisenhower and Vice President Richard Milhous Nixon.

August 23 Federal Reserve Board authorized an increase from 2¾ to 3% in the discount rate to be charged to member banks by Federal Reserve Banks in four areas, including New York.

September 7 Sherman Minton announced his retirement as Associate Justice of the Supreme Court, effective October 15.

October 12 Named Bertram D. Tallamy of New York to new post of Federal Highway Administrator.

October 16 Appointed William Joseph Brennan, Jr. of New Jersey Associate Justice of the Supreme Court.

October 23 Beginning of Hungarian revolt. Finally, on November 4, Russian troops attacked Budapest, crushing the revolt.

October 31 Anglo-French-Israeli forces attacked Eygpt. President Eisenhower announced his opposition to the use of force as an instrument for settlement of international disputes. Yielding to American pressure and Russian threats of intervention, British Prime Minister Anthony Eden announced that a cease-fire would begin at midnight, November 5.

November 2 Offered $20 million worth of food and medical supplies to Hungary.

November 6 National elections. Dwight D. Eisenhower reelected President. Eisenhower received 35,581,003 votes winning 457 electoral votes, and Adlai E. Stevenson received 26,031,322 votes winning 73 electoral votes.

November 8 United States offered to admit Hungarian refugees of anti-Soviet revolt.

November 17 Approved new regulations permitting United States Atomic Energy Commission to make uranium available to nations desiring it for nuclear reactors dedicated to peaceful uses.

November 27 Issued a statement reaffirming United States friendship with Britain and France.

December 2 Fidel Castro led small revolutionary expedition into Cuba. He gained more and more adherents until he finally forced President Fulgencio Batista to resign January 1, 1959.

December 6   President Eisenhower ordered air-and-sea lift to bring 21,500 Hungarian refugees to the United States by January 1, 1957, or shortly thereafter.

1957

January 1   In a letter to Soviet Premier Nikolai A. Bulganin, President Eisenhower emphasized that the United States preferred to continue disarmament negotiations within the framework of the United Nations.

January 5   Proposed the Eisenhower Doctrine, warning the Communist powers in an address to Congress that the United States would permit no further Communist conquests in the Middle East.

January 13-15   Took three-day tour of drought stricken areas of the Southwest and Mid-west.

SECOND TERM IN OFFICE

January 21   Formally inaugurated for second term. Oath administered by Chief Justice Earl Warren. (Took oath of office in private ceremony on Sunday, January 20).

January 28   Delivered special message to Congress proposing federal grant-in-aid program of $1.3 billion for school construction.

January 31   Urged Congress to enact legislation permitting more escapees from Communist-dominated countries to ˙enter the United States and liberalizing of Immigration and Nationality Act of 1952.

February 17   Publicly refused to grant any more concessions to Israel as a precondition to the withdrawal of its troops from the Gulf of Aqaba and the Gaza Strip.

February 20   Warned Israel in a nation-wide radio and television address that the United Nations had no choice but to exert pressure to force withdrawal from Egyptian territory.

February 28   Vice President Richard Nixon left Washington, D.C. for a 22-day tour of Italy and 8 African states.

March 9   Signed Eisenhower Doctrine bill authorizing the use of United States forces to assist Middle East nations threatened by Communist aggression.

March 14   Left Norfolk, Virginia, aboard guided missile cruiser *Canberra* for a voyage to Bermuda for conference with British Prime Minister Harold Macmillan.

March 24   President Eisenhower and Prime Minister Harold Macmillan issued a joint communique after their conference at Bermuda, stating that the United States agreed to supply guided missiles to Great Britain.

March 25   Appointed Charles Evans Whittaker of Missouri Associate Justice of the Supreme Court.

April 6   Vice President Nixon, in a report on his trip to Africa, proposed a broad program for assisting African countries in their struggle for political and economic advancement.

April 11   President Eisenhower, in a special message to Congress, proposed creation of a 3-member airways modernization board to work out improved air-tarffic control and air-navigation procedures.

April 12   Signed bill permitting the United States to cooperate in building an experimental power plant in West Berlin.

April 13   Postmaster General Arthur E. Summerfield ordered halting of normal Saturday mail deliveries and closing of post offices because of failure of Congress to appropriate supplemental funds for the remainder of the fiscal year. These funds were granted in a bill signed by President Eisenhower on April 16. The Postmaster General then ordered resumption of normal Saturday mail delivery.

April 20   Signed bill authorizing increase from 3% to 3¼% in the interest rate on two series of United States savings bonds.

April 29   Secretary of the Army Brucker dedicated Army's first nuclear power reactor at Fort Belvoir, Virginia.

May 14   United States resumed military aid to Yugoslavia which had been halted during Tito's reconciliation with the U.S.S.R.

Warned the nation that severe cuts in his defense budget might be a "needless gamble" with the safety of the United States.

May 15   Great Britain successfully tested a hydrogen bomb.

May 29   Accepted resignation of Secretary of the Treasury George M. Humphrey.

June 3-6   United States formally joined the Military Committee of the Baghdad Pact at a meeting of the Council of Ministers in Karachi.

June 5   President Eisenhower stated at a press conference that a total and complete ban on nuclear tests must await a firm and enforceable agreement with the U.S.S.R.

June 28   Secretary of Defense Charles Wilson with President Eisenhower's approval ordered a reduction of 100,000 men in the United States armed forces by the end of 1957.

July 3   Rejected proposals of opponents of civil rights bill that it be submitted to the people in a national referendum.

July 16   Secretary of Defense Charles Wilson with President Eisenhower's approval ordered a reduction of 100,000 men in the United States armed forces by the end of 1957.

July 20   Appointed committee of federal officials to cooperate with a committee of state governors in reappraising federal-state functions.

July 29   United States ratified International Atomic Energy Agency (proposed by President Eisenhower in 1953) to pool atomic resources for peaceful use.

Appointed Robert Bernard Anderson of Texas Secretary of the Treasury.

August 5   Stated in his first report to Congress on his Middle East doctrine that it had helped to achieve progress toward stability there.

August 12   Signed bill authorizing New York State to construct a $600 million power plant at Niagara Falls.

August 13   Signed bill authorizing the sale for foreign currencies of additional $1 billion in United States farm surpluses.

August 18   Following the signing of treaties of cooperation between the United States and Turkey, Iran, and Pakistan, and the withdrawal of Iraq, the Baghdad Pact was officially changed to the Central Treaty Organization (CENTO).

August 21   Announced United States offer to suspend nuclear weapons tests for two years in return for a Soviet agreement to a halt in production of fissionable material for weapons and to the establishment of an inspection system.

September 3   Signed bill authorizing death penalty for persons causing death by mailing explosives or poison.

September 4   Arkansas Governor Orval E. Faubus ordered National Guardsmen to bar nine Negro students from a high school in Little Rock.

September 9   Signed first Civil Rights Act since 1875, establishing 6-man bi-partisan commission with power to investigate all matters pertaining to denial of rights based on color, race, religion, and national origin.

     Maine voters approved constitutional amendment changing state's election date from September to November as in the other 47 states.

September 14   Conferred with Governor Faubus of Arkansas at Newport, Rhode Island, on the question of school integration.

September 20   Governor Faubus of Arkansas removed national guardsmen from Little Rock Central High School in compliance with a federal court injunction.

September 24 President Eisenhower sent frederal troops to Little Rock High School to enforce integration of Negro students.

September 26 First President to submerge in an atomic-powered submarine, the *Seawolf* off Newport, Rhode Island.

October 2 White House issued statement warning that final orders of United States Courts to end public school segregation had to be obeyed.

October 4 Launching of first Soviet Sputnik set off demand for greater American efforts in defense and technology.

October 8 Issued statement expressing concern that the United States was no further advanced in production of Intercontinental Ballistic Missiles.

Confessed spy Jack Soble sentenced in New York to 7-year imprisonment for espionage.

October 23 Accepted resignation of Attorney-General Herbert Brownell, Jr. Announced that William P. Rogers of New York would succeed him.

October 23-25 Prime Minister Harold Macmillan of Great Britain and President Eisenhower had 3-day conference in Washington, D.C.

October 30 Signed executive order specifying that states would not be entitled to federal disaster relief unless they gave assurance that they would spend a reasonable amount of their own funds.

November 1 Pennsylvania Railroad and New York Central jointly announced that they were considering the possibility of a merger.

November 7 Delivered nationwide radio and television address to allay fears concerning Soviet scientific achievements.

Named the six members of the newly created Civil Rights Commission with retired Supreme Court Justice Stanley F. Reed as Chairman.

November 13 Proposed in nationwide address a considerable increase in defense spending to meet the challenge of scientific advances by the U.S.S.R.

November 25 White House announced recess appointment of Assistant Attorney-General W. Wilson White as Chief of the newly created Civil Rights Division of the Justice Department.

November 26 Suffered mild stroke from which he recovered rapidly.

December 10 President Eisenhower's physicians announced that he was physically fit to attend the meeting of NATO heads of government in Paris.

December 15 Rejected an appeal by Indian Prime Minister Nehru for a halt in nuclear weapons tests.

December 16-19 Attended heads of government conference of NATO in Paris, France. A final communique was issued· indicating increased emphasis on the political aims of NATO.

December 17 United States successfully fired for the first time the Atlas Intercontinental Ballistic Missile.

December 23 Delivered a nationwide radio and television report on the NATO Conference indicating that the U.S.S.R. must show a new attitude if the impasse over arms control is to be ended.

December 20 Marion B. Folsom, Secretary of Health, Education, and Welfare, announced a four-year $1 billion administration program to meet emergency needs in United States education.

1958

January 3 United States Air Force announced formation of the first two squadrons and with intermediate-range ballistic missiles under the Strategic Air Command.

January 7 Requested that Congress appropriate an additional $1,370,-000,000 in fiscal 1958 to speed up and expand missile and air defenses.

January 12 Stated in letter to Soviet Premier Nikolai A. Bulganin his willingness to participate in a summit conference if agenda was prepared in advance by other officials and offered good hope of advancing peace and justice.

Publication of the *Daily Worker,* the United States Communist newspaper, was suspended because of declining revenues.

January 16 Secretary of State John Foster Dulles urged formation of international commission to control outer space and insure its use for peaceful purposes.

January 23 In a special message to Congress, President Eisenhower recommended enactment of legislation to end corruption in the ranks of labor.

January 27 Urged enactment of an "emergency" four-year program to improve education, especially in mathematics and science.

January 28 Appointed William Pierce Rogers of New York Attorney General.

January 30 Requested Congress to extend the reciprocal trade program for five years beyond June 30, 1958.

February 7 Department of Defense formally established the Advanced Research Projects Agency to take charge of missile and related programs with Roy W. Johnson as director.

February 22 In a television address former President Harry S Truman charged the Eisenhower Administration with bringing on the recession and with inadvertently helping the Soviets.

United States and Great Britain signed five-year agreement for supplying of United States intermediate-range ballistic missiles to Britain.

February 26 President Eisenhower stated that he had a clear understanding with Vice President Nixon on what should be done if the President became incapacitated.

February 27 Signed bill temporarily raising national debt limit from $275 to $285 billion.

March 5 Vetoed Congressional appropriation to make the United States the first nation to put a nuclear powered airplane in the air, claiming that scarce talent would be wasted if the United States concentrated only on a prestige object.

March 25 Urged Congressional approval of temporary continuation of unemployment compensation to those who had exhausted their state benefits.

March 26 Announced that the United States would invite foreign scientists, including some from Communist countries, to observe forthcoming United States nuclear tests in the Pacific.

March 27 Russian Premier Nikolai Bulganin resigned. Nikita S. Khrushchev, Secretary of the Communist Party was elected Premier. On March 31 Khrushchev announed unilateral suspension of nuclear tests by the U.S.S.R.

March 31 Vetoed bill to freeze farm price supports and acreage allotments of 1957 levels for one year.

April 1 Signed first anti-recession legislation: Emergency Housing Bill to stimulate housing construction by calling for federal purchase of new home mortgages and providing additional money for federal loans on veterans' housing.

April 2 Asked Congress to authorize establishment of a national aeronautics and space agency to administer nonmilitary space research and exploration projects.

April 16 Signed bill extending exemption from admission taxes to dramatic and musical performances by non-profit civic groups, as well as to athletic games, if proceeds were divided among sponsoring educational institutions and hospitals for crippled children.

April 24 Sent to Congress plan for merging of Federal Civil Defense Administration and Office of Defense Mobilization.

April 28 Sent letter to Soviet Premier Nikita Khrushchev asking his government to support the United States proposal for arctic inspection plan to allay fear of surprise attack.

May 8   Ordered federalized National Guardsmen withdrawn from Central High School, Little Rock.

May 20   Delivered nationwide radio and television address stating that an economic upturn was in the making and promised early decision on proposed tax reductions.

May 26   Asked Congress not to reduce excise and corporation income taxes, but to extend existing rates for one year.

May 27   Signed bill, effective August 1, 1958, increasing postal workers' pay and increasing postal rates.

May 30   Two American Unknown Soldiers of World War II buried in Arlington National Cemetery.

June 4   Signed bill authorizing the Federal Government to advance money to states to continue compensation to jobless workers who had used up their state unemployment benefits.

June 13   Requested Congress to establish federal aviation agency to (1) absorb the Civil Aeronautics Administration and the Airways Modernization Board, (2) issue safety rules, and (3) assume certain defense department functions.

June 17   Presidential Assistant Sherman Adams denied before a House Investigating Committee that he had intervened with federal agencies on behalf of industrialist Bernard Goldfine. President Eisenhower indicated his support for Adams on June 18. Sherman Adams finally resigned on September 22 after Republicans pressured him because of their fear that he was endangering GOP chances in the November elections.

June 20   Signed bill raising salaries of over one million federal employees by 10%, retroactive to January 1, 1958.

July 2   Signed bill permitting the United States to share with its allies previously restricted nuclear information, designs and materials.

July 7   Signed bill requiring automobile manufacturers to affix retail price tags to new cars.

Signed bill for Alaskan statehood.

July 8-11   Made visit to Canada to explore ways to improve United States-Canadian relations.

July 12-   Sent Milton Eisenhower on goodwill mission to Central
August 1   America. He reported the need for closer economic and political cooperation, including financial aid to Central America.

July 15   United States Marines landed in Lebanon in response to request from President Camille Chamoun for assistance under the Eisenhower Doctrine. (Revolt had broken out May 9). Troops were gradually removed during October.

Signed act, with "misgivings," for subsidized construction of a sister liner of the *United States* and one other superliner.

July 29   Signed bill creating the National Aeronautics and Space Administration (NASA) to direct United States nonmilitary space activities.

August 1   Appointed Arthur Sherwood Flemming of Ohio, Secretary of Health, Education, and Welfare.

New postal rates into effect. Regular mail rose from 3¢ to 4¢ an ounce, domestic airmail from 6¢ to 7¢.

August 4   Vetoed Independent Offices Appropriations bill for fiscal 1959 on the basis of an unjustifiable authorization of a $584 million payment into the United States Civil Service Retirement fund.

August 6   Signed Defense Reorganization Act which set up a plan to subordinate the uniformed services to a central civilian authority.

August 12   Signed bill curbing the right of federal agencies to withhold information from the public.

Signed bill making it easier for railroads to obtain loans, raise rates, and abandon unprofitable lines.

August 13   Delivered personal address to a special session of the United Nations General Assembly, presenting a six-point plan for peace in the Middle East.

August 25   Signed Presidential Pensions bill granting pensions to ex-Presidents of the United States. First such act providing pensions for former Chief Executives.

Signed Budget Reform bill giving Congress closer control over federal spending.

August 27   Signed bill for the humane slaughtering of livestock in processing houses.

August 28   Signed Agricultural bill which modified price supports on basic crops for 1959 and 1960, giving the farmers a choice between modified price supports and an increase of crop allotments.

Signed Labor Pension Reporting bill which required the reporting and disclosure of employee welfare and pension plans which covered more than 25 employees whether managed by unions or employers.

September 2   Signed National Defense Education Act which established a $295 million loan fund for college students. Loans with 3% interest over 10 years with 50% reduction if students taught in elementary or secondary schools for five years.

Signed Excise Tax Technical Changes bill which made the first important revision since 1932 of the general excise tax provisions of the Internal Revenue Code.

September 6   Signed Food and Drug Cosmetic Act amendment requiring food manufacturers to prove the chemical additives they use in food are safe.

September 9   Ordered federal agencies to cut their employment levels by 2% in fiscal 1959 to absorb a pay raise voted by Congress.

September 11 Delivered radio and television address stating that the United States would defend Quemoy and Matsu from Chinese Communist aggression.

September 14   Signed Labor Management Reporting and Disclosure bill designed to suppress gangsterism, racketeering, and blackmail in labor organizations.

September 30   Appointed Lieutenant Elwood R. Quesada as administrator of the new Federal Aviation Agency.

October 2   U.S.S.R. announced that it had resumed testing of nuclear weapons.

October 7   Appointed Potter Stewart of Ohio as Associate Justice of the Supreme Court.

October 12   Ordered the Federal Bureau of Investigation to investigate an explosion which wrecked a Jewish Temple in Atlanta, Georgia.

October 30   United States and Great Britain announced suspension of nuclear tests, effective October 31, for at least one year which the U.S.S.R. ignored in continuing its current series of tests.

November 4   National elections. Resounding defeat for Republicans in both Houses of Congress. President Eisenhower in a news conference on November 5 blamed this defeat on voter apathy toward the great danger of reckless federal spending.

November 8   United States and Euratom signed an agreement to stimulate nuclear power production in the community and to share the resulting technical experience.

November 10   Sinclair Weeks resigned as Secretary of Commerce.

November 24   Appointed a nonpartisan 9-man Committee headed by William H. Draper to make a critical appraisal of United States expenditures abroad for military assistance and economic aid.

December 1   Directed the National Science Foundation to set up an information service to index the growing volume of scientific information in the United States and abroad.

December 14   United States, Great Britain, and France formally rejected Soviet demands for withdrawal from West Berlin.

December 20   Approved a new design for the reverse of the Lincoln penny as a feature of the observation in 1959 of the sesquicentennial of Lincoln's birth.

December 27   White House announced creation of new interdepartmental council for science and technology, headed by James R. Killian, Jr.

1959

January 3   Proclaimed Alaska the 49th state.

January 5   White House released statement from science advisory committee questioning the reliability of detecting underground nuclear test explosions by methods proposed at the 1958 Geneva conference of nuclear experts.

January 23   Designated flood-stricken portions of Ohio and Pennsylvania as federal disaster areas.

January 27   Submitted 20-point labor program to Congress in a special message which was designed to curb recently revealed abuses in collective bargining.

January 29   Urged Congress to abandon mandatory high farm price supports in a special message.

January 31   Named Vice President Richard M. Nixon chairman of a permanent cabinet committee on price stability for economic growth.

February 2   Outlined to Congress a 10-year space program to launch a satellite'or space-probe vehicle each month starting in mid-1959.

February 4   After being detained 54 hours, four United States army trucks crossed into West Berlin from East Germany at Helmstedt without Russian inspection.

February 5   Submitted a 7-point civil rights program in special message to Congress, including support and encouragement for school integration.

February 19   Arrived in Acapulco, Mexico, for a visit with Mexican President Lopez Mateos.

March 16   Indicated willingness to attend a summit conference with the U.S.S.R. if preliminary negotiations proved promising.

March 18   Signed bill admitting Hawaii as the 50th state.

March 23   Signed bill for extension of the peacetime draft to July 1, 1963.

March 30   The Supreme Court in *Abbatev v. U.S.* (359 U.S. 187) and *Bartkis v. Illinois* (359 U.S. 121) upheld double jeopardy permitting a person to be tried for the same offense in federal and state courts.

March 31   Signed bill providing for limited 3-month extension of emergency federal employment compensation program.

April 4   Delivered address at Gettysburg College in Pennsylvania, insisting that foreign aid was essential to frustrate the Communist goal of world domination.

April 8   National Aeronautics and Space Administration (NASA) presented to Congress a long-range program for exploration of space.

April 15   Secretary of State John Foster Dulles resigned due to incapacitating illness.

April 16   United States and U.S.S.R. agreed in Washington, D.C., to exchange performing artists in connection with 1959 national exhibitions to be held in Moscow and New York.

April 18   Nominated Christian Archibald Herter of Massachusetts as Secretary of State. The Senate waived the 7-day interval between introduction and confirmation of a presidential appointment and confirmed the appointment in 4½ hours.

May 11   Urged Congressional approval of United States membership in Inter-American Development Bank.

May 20   Conferred the Medal of Freedom, highest United States civilian award, on John Foster Dulles.

May 24   Former Secretary of State John Foster Dulles died of cancer. President Eisenhower ordered an official funeral with full military honors.

June 8   Urged Congress in a special message to abolish interest ceiling on United States savings and treasury bonds and to raise the public debt limit to $295 billion.

June 11   Advised Congress of plans to send atomic weapons to Greece and to train Greek troops in their use.

June 15   Federal Communications Commission affirmed its ruling that radio and television stations must give "equal time" to political candidates on news programs as well as in actual political debate.

June 17   Refused personal or federal agency intervention in the steel industry wage negotiations.

June 18   President Eisenhower suffered his first rejection of a nominee for a Cabinet post when the Senate refused to confirm the appointment of Lewis L. Strauss as Secretary of Commerce. Opposition to Strauss was due to his supposed high-handed methods as Chairman of the Atomic Energy Commission.

June 23   General Maxwell Taylor resigned as Army Chief. He stated that his decision had been influenced by rejection of his efforts to modernize the Army.

June 24   President Eisenhower requested Congress to approve "permanent" instead of annual legislative authority for foreign military aid.

June 26   Formally dedicated St. Lawrence Seaway with Queen Elizabeth II.

June 27   United States denounced Cuba before the Organization of American States as contributing to Caribbean tensions and for its slanderous attacks upon the United States.

June 29   Signed bill authorizing $126 million for a two-year extension of the federal-aid-to-airport-development program.

June 30   Signed bill raising temporary debt limit to $295 billion and the permanent limit to $285 billion.

July 6   Ordered reduction of quota of Cuban sugar to be imported into the United States by 700,000 pounds.

July 7   Vetoed an omnibus housing bill because it was excessive, defective, inflationary, and an obstacle to constructive progress toward better housing for Americans.

July 24   Vice President Richard Nixon, on official visit to Russia, opened the American Exhibition in Moscow after a "debate" with Soviet Premier Nikita Khrushchev in the Kitchen Exhibit.

Federal Communications Commission ordered $50 million per year reduction in long-distance phone rates.

July 28   Signed bill to relax severe restrictions governing member banks of Federal Reserve System.

August 1   Vice President Nixon in radio-television address from Moscow told the Soviet people that they would continue to live in an era of fear, suspicion, and tension if Premier Khrushchev tried to promote communization of countries outside the U.S.S.R.

August 3   President Eisenhower announced that Soviet Premier Khrushchev would visit the United States in September, 1959, and that he would make a trip to the U.S.S.R. later in the year.

August 6   Delivered radio-television address to the nation calling for an effective labor reform law to drive corrupt elements from the labor-management field.

Signed bill authorizing Tennessee Valley Authority to sell $750 million in revenue bonds to cover construction of power projects.

August 7   Signed bill for United States participation in Inter-American Development Bank.

August 10 Appointed Frederick Henry Mueller of Michigan Secretary of Commerce.

August 21 Officially proclaimed Hawaii the 50th State of the Union.

August 25 Sent special messages to Congress requesting removal of interest ceilings on long-term government bonds, extension of Federal Housing Authority home loan insurance, and an increased federal tax on motor fuels.

August 25-
September 7 Visited Germany, England, and France.

August 26 State Department announced extension of United States nuclear test ban from October 31 to December 31, 1959.

August 29 Signed pension revision bill to increase veterans' pensions for non-service connected disabilities.

September 7 Civil Rights Commission requested President Eisenhower to appoint federal registrars to supervise in areas where local officials had prevented Negroes from voting.

September 9 Vetoed Public Works bill. On September 10 the Congress overrode President Eisenhower's veto for the first time.

In a radio-television address President Eisenhower termed Soviet recognition of allied rights a key condition for a summit meeting.

September 13 Signed Medical Care bill which created a federal-state medical care program for the needy aged, with federal contributions granted to existing state medical-care programs for needy persons 65 and over, as well as funds on a matching basis to help start new programs.

September 14 Signed bill exempting radio and television news of political candidates from FCC "equal time" requirements in case where one candidate had appeared in a newscast, news interview, news documentary, or on-the-spot news coverage.

Signed Labor Reform bill of 1959.

Signed bill including "modern" works among the art objects that may be imported duty-free.

Signed bill barring states from taxing incomes of out-of-state firms net through business done in a state in which they maintain no facilities.

September 15-27 Soviet Premier Nikita Khrushchev visited the United States, conferring with President Eisenhower at Camp David, Maryland, September 25-27.

September 16 President Eisenhower pocket-vetoed a bill to create a coal research and development commission because it threatened to dilute the Interior Department's responsibility and to blur "lines of governmental responsibility."

September 17 Secretary of State Christian Herter delivered address before the United States General Assembly appealing to the U.S.S.R. to join in a new attempt to control the arms race.

September 19 President Eisenhower publicly criticized the first session of the 86th Congress as a disappointing failure, especially indicating its "extravagant proposals" and the "short-sighted cuts in military outlay."

September 21 Signed bill increasing federal taxes on gasoline by 1¢ per gallon effective October 1 in order to finance the national highway program.

September 22 Signed bill authorizing a New York-New Jersey Transportation Agency under a compact already ratified by both states for handling bi-state commuter traffic problems.

September 23 Signed housing bill providing $1 billion for construction and mortgages. The FHA immediately invoked the bill's authority to increase interest rates from 5¼% to 5¾% on home mortgages issued by it.

October 9 Invoked Taft-Hartley Act in the steel strike, naming a board to inquire into the dispute.

October 12 Embargo placed on all products except medical supplies and food to the island of Cuba.

October 13 Broke ground for Dwight D. Eisenhower Library at Abilene, Kansas.

Proposed in television address that money saved by global disarmament could be used to raise living standards in under-developed countries.

October 19 United States Development Loan Fund announced in a major policy statement that future loans to underdeveloped countries must be spent for United States goods.

October 21 President Eisenhower approved plans for transfer to NASA of army ballistic missile agency and its space team headed by Werhner von Braun.

October 26 Announced firm intention of the administration to defend United States Naval base at Guantanamo, Cuba.

October 29 Approved New York City site for a 1964 World's Fair.

November 9 Secretary of State Christian Herter disclosed that the United States had agreed to closer cooperation with the rest of NATO in plans for negotiations with the U.S.S.R.

November 14 Announced establishment of a national advisory committee on inter-American affairs.

November 21 Named General W. B. Palmer to new position as military foreign aid director.

November 30 United States, Great Britain, and U.S.S.R. agreed on details for a central organization to be set up, with signing of nuclear test ban treaty.

December 2 Announced at his press conference that American foreign aid would not be used for promotion of birth control in underdeveloped areas.

December 3 F. M. Eaton of New York was named chairman of the United States delegation to a ten-nation disarmament committee to meet in Geneva early in 1960.

December 3-22 President Eisenhower visited 11 nations in Europe, Asia, and Africa.

December 20   Soviet Premier Nikita Khrushchev was invited by President Eisenhower, British Prime Minister Harold Macmillan, French President Charles deGaulle, and German Chancellor Konrad Adenauer to attend summit talks in Paris to start on April 25, 1960.

December 23   President Eisenhower stated in nation-wide radio-television address that he had found a deep hunger for peace wherever he went in his 11-nation tour.

December 25   Soviet Premier Khrushchev accepted the West's invitation for a summit conference, suggesting April 21, or May 4, 1960.

December 29   President Eisenhower announced that the United States was reserving the right to resume nuclear tests after December 31, 1959.

December 30   Soviet Premier Khrushchev accepted the United States, British and French proposal for a summit meeting in Paris, May 16, 1960.

1960

January 13   Appealed to Congress in a special message for removal of 4¼% ceiling on interest on long-term treasury bonds.

January 14   Informed Congress that he was transferring army ballistic missile agency under Wernher von Braun to civilian controlled National Aeronautics and Space Administration.

January 19   United States and Japanese Governments signed Mutual Security Treaty under which both countries pledged to maintain and develop their capacities to resist armed attacks.

January 26   In a formal restatement of United States policy President Eisenhower reaffirmed that there would be no reprisals against Cuba or intervention in its internal affairs.

February 16   France successfully tested an atomic bomb.

February 20   President Eisenhower issued an Executive Order establishing new industrial security program enlarging the right of accused security risks to confront and cross-examine their accusers.

February 22-
March 7
Embarked on an extended Latin-American tour.

February 23
Vetoed bill to increase efforts to clear river pollution because of excessive demand for federal funds.

February 29
Supreme Court unanimously reversed decision of United States District court in Georgia, which had held as unconstitutional a provision of the 1957 Civil Rights Act permitting the Justice Department to bring civil suits in behalf of persons deprived of their voting rights.

March 8
Delivered nationwide radio and television address asserting that with few exceptions United States relations with Latin America had reached their highest point.

March 11
Sent special message to Congress urging that higher postal rates be authorized.

March 15
Met with West German Chancellor Konrad Adenauer at the White House assuring him of United States support in maintaining the freedom of West Berlin.

March 15-
June 27
Ten-Nation Disarmament Conference remained deadlocked over controls and compliance.

March 16
Endorsed Vice President Richard M. Nixon as his successor.

March 17
Urged Congress in special message to double number of quota immigrants accepted by the United States each year.

March 28
Began talks with British Prime Minister Harold Macmillan at Camp David, Maryland, primarily concerned with the negotiations for suspension of nuclear tests.

April 1
18th decennial census of the United States was begun.

April 18
Approved a nine-point program for improvement of relations between the United States and Panama vis-a-vis the Canal Zone.

Made public his offer to give the Government the bulk of his personal and state papers—to be deposited at the Dwight D. Eisenhower Library at Abilene, Kansas.

April 22　French President Charles deGaulle arrived in Washington, D.C. on a state visit to the United States.

President Eisenhower created a three-man emergency board under the Railway Labor Act to investigate a dispute between the major railroads and 11 nonoperating railroad unions.

Cuban Premier Fidel Castro charged in a television speech that the United States was plotting to overthrow his government.

May 1-11　U-2 incident. U.S.S.R. announced on May 5, the shooting down of an American U-2. After first denying its intelligence mission the United States admitted on May 7 that the U-2 shot down was on such a mission. President Eisenhower announced on May 11 that he had authorized the U-2 mission. The Soviet Union cancelled an invitation to the President to visit the country.

May 2　Appealed to the nation to exert influence in persuading Congress not to cut his foreign aid proposals.

May 4　United States and India signed four-year agreement in Washington, D.C., for purchase by India of 17 million metric tons of United States surplus grain.

May 6　Signed Civil Rights Act of 1960.

May 7　Announced that the United States planned to resume underground nuclear testing as part of research on the detection of such blasts.

May 13　Vetoed bill authorizing federal loans and grants to economically depressed areas.

May 16-17　Summit Conference of Heads of State of France, United States, Great Britain, and Soviet Union opened in Paris. Premier Khrushchev declared that President Eisenhower would not be welcome in the U.S.S.R. President Eisenhower announced suspension of United States reconnaissance flights over the U.S.S.R.

May 18 Premier Khrushchev's press conference threatened "devastating" blows against bases used by United States reconnaissance plans. The U.S.S.R. requested meeting of the United Nations Security Council to examine Soviet charges concerning flights of such planes.

May 20 Federal Communications Commission announced program to supervise the content of radio and television programs.

May 23 UN Security Council opened debate on Soviet charges of United States aggression through the flight of United States planes over Soviet territory. On May 26 the Council rejected a Soviet resolution to condemn United States for acts of aggression against the U.S.S.R.

May 25 In a radio and television address, President Eisenhower stated that in spite of the failure of the Summit Conference the United States must continue businesslike dealings with the Soviet leadership.

May 27 Announced termination of United States economic aid to Cuba.

June 2 Federal reserve board authorized reduction in discount rate from 4 to 3½% by two federal reserve banks.

June 12 Began tour of Far East.

June 16 Cancelled proposed trip to Japan because of security risks created by Japanese riots.

June 20 Supreme Court ruled that the Civil Rights Commission had power to subpoena voting registrars and compel them to testify without giving it the names of persons charging voting irregularities.

June 22	United States-Japanese security treaty ratified by Senate (ratified by Japan on June 19 after anti-American riots had caused cancellation of President Eisenhower's visit). Treaty into force on June 23.
July 1	House of Representatives and Senate overrode President Eisenhower's veto of a bill providing pay increases for federal employees.
July 4	New 50 star United States flag officially flown for the first time.
July 7	Nearly all Cuban sugar imports prohibited.
July 9	Warned that the United States would never permit establishment in the Western Hemisphere of a regime dominated by international communism.
July 11	Outlined plan for coordinated Western Hemispheric aid to Latin America, including government aid and private investment.
July 11-14	Democratic National Convention at Los Angeles, California, nominated Senator John Fitzgerald Kennedy of Massachusetts for President and Senator Lyndon Baines Johnson of Texas for Vice President.
July 12	Soviet Premier Khrushchev declared at a news conference in Moscow that the Monroe Doctrine was dead and that the U.S.S.R. would support Cuba in an effort to eliminate the United States Naval Base at Guantanamo. The United States State Department responded on July 14 by reaffirming the principles of the Monroe Doctrine.
July 14	Signed bill providing for Commerce Department registration of the names of drivers whose licenses were revoked for drunken driving or for traffic violations involving loss of life.
	Signed bill authorizing Post Office Department to file for court orders to impound the mail of persons believed to be sources of pornography.
July 22	Ordered a 3% reduction in the number of federal employees.

July 25-28　　Republican National Convention at Chicago, Illinois, nominated Vice President Richard M. Nixon for President and Senator Henry Cabot Lodge of Massachusetts for Vice President.

July 28　　The three major television networks offered to give the two major party candidates free prime evening time for a series of face-to-face debates on campaign issues. Democratic nominee John F. Kennedy accepted the same day, and Republican nominee Richard M. Nixon agreed on July 31.

August 3　　Vice President Richard M. Nixon opened Presidential campaign with visit to Hawaii.

August 10　　Senate ratified 12-nation treaty dedicating Antarctica to peaceful pursuits.

August 19　　Francis Gary Powers, pilot of U-2 flight downed in U.S.S.R. was found guilty by a Soviet military tribunal of charges of espionage for the United States and was sentenced to ten years "loss of liberty."

August 24　　President Eisenhower signed bill suspending equal-time requirement for political radio and television broadcasts by presidential and vice presidential candidates during the 1960 campaign.

September 7　　Ordered that Panamanian and American flags should both be flown in the Canal Zone after mobs had attacked the United States Embassy in Panama City on September 3.

September 9　　Signed bill appropriating $500,000,000 for social and economic aid to Latin America and $100 million for earthquake relief in Chile.

September 13　　Signed bill to curb radio-television payola and tighten restrictions on other deceptive broadcasting practices.

Signed bill establishing a program for federal-state medical care for the aged and to make other social security liberalizations.

September 20 Opening of United Nations General Assembly in New York attended by world leaders.

September 22 President Eisenhower delivered address to UN General Assembly appealing to all nations to join in settling world problems by negotiations and cooperation in the United Nations.

September 26 First of a series of television debates between Republican Presidential nominee Richard M. Nixon and Democratic nominee John F. Kennedy took place in Chicago, Illinois.

October 1 Soviet Premier Nikita Khrushchev warned the UN General Assembly that only the admission of Communist China to the United Nations could avert the danger of atomic war.

October 2 President Eisenhower rejected proposal made by five neutralist leaders that he meet with Premier Khrushchev.

October 7 Second television debate between Presidential candidates John F. Kennedy and Richard M. Nixon. They disagreed sharply as to whether the United States should defend the Chinese off shore islands of Quemoy and Matsu.

October 17 National variety store chains: Woolworth, Kressge, W. T. Grant, and McCrory-McLellan announced that lunch counters in their stores had been integrated in more than 100 southern cities.

October 19 President Eisenhower announced that Canada and the United States had negotiated a ten-year agreement relating to cooperative development of the water resources of the Columbia River basin.

October 20 State Department placed embargo on exports for Cuba except some medicine and foodstuffs.

October 28 United States Government requested the Organization of American States to investigate reports that Cuba was receiving large shipments of arms from the Soviet bloc.

November 1   President Eisenhower announced that appropriate steps would be taken to defend the United States naval base at Guantanamo, Cuba.

November 8   National elections. John Fitzerald Kennedy elected President. Kennedy received 34,221,531 votes winning 303 electoral votes. Richard M. Nixon received 34,108,474 votes winning 219 electoral votes.

November 14 President-elect Kennedy and Vice President Nixon conferred at Key Biscayne, Florida, in first post-election meeting.

November 16 President Eisenhower ordered all agencies to cut their spending abroad sharply as means of stemming the increasing deficit in the United States balance of payments.

November 19 Released report of his science advisory committee which urged the federal government and all other elements of the national community to assume a greater role in supporting, strengthening, and expanding basic scientific research and graduate education in science.

December 1   Authorized the expenditure of up to $1 million for relief of Cuban refugees in the United States.

December 5   Supreme Court ruled that racial discrimination in bus terminal restaurants serving passengers who cross state lines was a violation of the Interstate Commerce Act.

December 6   Conferred with President-Elect Kennedy at the White House on world problems.

December 14 Western European Nations and the United States and Canada signed an agreement in Paris for the creation of an Organization for Economic Cooperation and Development.

December 23 In his last Christmas message to the nation, President Eisenhower called for an end of racial discrimination and other national flaws.

December 29   Eisenhower administration was revealed to favor development and utilization of communications satellites by private industry.

1961

January 3   President Eisenhower severed diplomatic relations with Cuba.

January 6   Seven executives of electrical manufacturing companies jailed for antitrust violations.

January 14   Prohibited holding of gold abroad by United States citizens and corporations.

January 17   Delivered farewell address to the Nation urging vigilance against dangers to its liberties implicit in a vast military establishment.

            President Eisenhower and Canadian Prime Minister John G. Diefenbaker in Washington, D.C., signed Canadian-United States Treaty for joint development of Columbia River resources.

January 18   At his final press conference President Eisenhower urged a constitutional amendment decreasing the time between Presidential election and inauguration. His greatest regret was that he had not been able to establish permanent peace.

RETIREMENT

January 20   John F. Kennedy inaugurated as 35th President of the United States. Oath administered by Chief Justice Earl Warren.

March 22   Rank of 5-Star General restored to former President Eisenhower by Act signed by President Kennedy. Eisenhower was not to receive military pension because of Presidential pension. He and his wife, Mamie, entitled to military hospitalization benefits and space-available transportation.

June 15 Addressed opening session of world conference of Local Governments, indicating opposition to the mania of over-zealous central agencies which try to dominate rather than serve local government.

November 8 Appointed first chairman of board of trustees of a new people-to-people organization by President Kennedy. Idea was originated by Eisenhower.

November 10 Delivered address rededicating Liberty Memorial in Kansas City, Missouri, calling the people-to-people idea a better path to peace than government-to-government negotiation. Visited with Former President Harry S Truman in their first friendly meeting since coldness verging on animosity developed between the two men during the 1952 election campaign.

1962

January 12 Received intelligence briefing on current United States foreign affairs and security problems as part of regular briefings ordered by President Kennedy for him and former Presidents Herbert Hoover and Harry S Truman.

February 1 Appeared in closed-circuit television program for Republican rallies in 17 cities. Said GOP should welcome potential allies regardless of their political affiliations, encouraging groupings which support responsible progress.

March 24 Visited by President Kennedy to discuss the world situation in general.

May 1 Delivered speech dedicating Eisenhower Library at Abilene, Kansas, deploring the decline in American concept of beauty, decency, and morality during the period of scientific and industrial development.

May 10 At his first Washington news conference since he left the Presidency, Eisenhower warned that the efforts of the Kennedy Administration to increase the Executive power could erode "self-reliant citizenship" and pose a "threat to our liberties."

June 1	Criticized Kennedy Administration's reckless spending program which had been a basic cause of a lack of confidence in the nation's economy.
June 30	Met with 100 leading Republicans at his first All-Republican Conference at his Gettysburg, Pennsylvania farm. Eisenhower urged businessmen to participate in politics.
July 18-August 30	Toured 7 Western European nations with wife Mamie and two grandchildren, Dwight David Eisenhower, 2d and Barbara Anne Eisenhower. Was received by heads of state although this was a private visit.
August 5	Published article in *Saturday Evening Post* criticizing Administration for space program, greater centralization in Executive Branch, its farm program, and its tactics in the shed price controversy.
October 7-10	Toured ten states to campaign for GOP candidates including Richard M. Nixon's gubernatorial campaign in California.
October 29	Delivered address in Syracuse, New York, stating that his administration's accomplishments had provided the military readiness and legislative and political backing that made President Kennedy's actions possible.
November 17	Attended dedication ceremonies with President Kennedy for Dulles International Airport, 27 miles from Washington, D.C., in Virginia.
December 7	Addressed closing session of National Association of Manufacturers, criticizing the extension of Federal Government influence and power.

1963

January 26	Suggested in article in *Saturday Evening Post* that the tenure of Senators and Representatives be limited to twelve years.
March 11	Published *The Ordeal of Power*.

May 18   Charged the Kennedy administration with trying to commit the United States to a rising fiscal adventure and denounced deficit spending in an article in the *Saturday Evening Post.*

June 12   Met with President Kennedy as part of the latter's attempt to gain partisan and nationwide support for his civil rights program.

September 7   King Mohammed Zahir and Queen Hamaira of Afghanistan visited former President Eisenhower at his Gettysburg, Pennsylvania farm as part of their state visit to the United States.

October 5   Expressed support for sale of wheat to Russia.

October 8   Stated in an interview that he thought President Kennedy was reckless in budgetary affairs.

October 18   Published an article in the *Saturday Evening Post* urging withdrawal of some United States troops from Europe and insisting that European nations assume a larger share of the Western defense burden.

November 10   Appeared on "Face the Nation" Program stating that if a deadlock occurred at Republican Conventions Nixon would be one of the likely persons to be looked to because of his knowledge and courage.

November 17   In a taped interview on ABC-TV for "Issues and Answers" Eisenhower called for withdrawal of five of the six United States divisions in Europe, claiming that the situation had radically changed since 1951.

November 22   President John F. Kennedy was assassinated in Dallas, Texas, by Lee Harvey Oswald. Vice President Lyndon Baines Johnson was sworn in as the 36th President.

November 23   Conferred with President Johnson at the White House.

December 7   Published an article in the *Saturday Evening Post* proposing a change in the Presidential succession by eliminating the Speaker of the House of Representatives and the President pro tempore of the Senate, instead listing the Secretary of State and other Cabinet offices after the Vice-President.

1964

January 29   Delivered address to Republican "Go-Day Dinner via closed-circuit television suggesting that the Party establish a system of party-to-people panels to conduct forums throughout the country.

February 4   *Creative America* published in which Eisenhower contributed some essays.

February 21   President Johnson and President Lopez Mateos of Mexico paid a social call on Eisenhower at Palm Desert, California, as part of their 2-day series of conferences.

May 23   Attended dedication of George C. Marshall Research Library at the Virginia Military Institute in Lexington, Virginia.

May 25   Made statement for the New York *Herald Tribune* outlining the principles he hoped the Republican Presidential nominee would apply to the nation's problems, including a belief in limited government, maintaining peace while protecting and extending freedom, loyal support for the United Nations, and prudent foreign affairs action.

June 6   Called meeting at Gettysburg, Pennsylvania, with Pennsylvania Governor William Scranton. Eisenhower's call for an open convention was rumored to be an anti-Goldwater move although he had denied on June 1 that he was against Goldwater.

June 11   Indicated at an informal interview some reservations concerning Barry Goldwater as the Republican nominee because of his views concerning civil rights falling within the purview of the states, Goldwater's almost complete control of the Republican Convention, and Goldwater's foreign policy.

June 18   Senator Barry Goldwater visited former President Eisenhower to explain his views on the Civil Rights Bill although he felt that it was not in accord with the Constitution.

July 13-16   Republican National Convention at San Francisco, California, nominated Barry M. Goldwater of Arizona for President and Representative William E. Miller of New York for Vice President.

Former President Eisenhower who attended the convention as a commentator for ABC Television Network addressed the Convention on July 14 calling for party unity and stricter local action to combat lawlessness and school segregation problems.

August 12 Attended Republican Unity Conference with Republican Presidential nominee Barry M. Goldwater, 14 Republican Governors and other Republican leaders. Eisenhower stated at a news conference after the meeting that Senator Goldwater had clarified certain views, and he was now happy with him as the candidate.

August 24-27 Democratic National Convention at Atlantic City, New Jersey, renominated President Lyndon B. Johnson and nominated Senator Hubert H. Humphrey of Minnesota for Vice President.

September 22 Taped television conversation between Senator Goldwater and Ex-President Eisenhower broadcast as a political message on NBC-TV indicating that Goldwater was not a war monger.

October 5 Republican task force report issued criticizing overextension of Presidential control of nuclear weapons. Eisenhower indicated to the press that he did not feel that the use of nuclear weapons should be a campaign issue.

October 14 Eisenhower declined the possibility of his being sent to survey the situation in Vietnam if Goldwater were elected President.

November 3 National elections. President Johnson reelected. President Johnson received 43,121,085 votes winning 486 electoral votes. Senator Goldwater received 27,145,161 votes winning 52 electoral votes.

December 9 Met with Senator Goldwater and former Vice President Richard M. Nixon in New York for private conference on the Party's position.

December 10 Suggested a two-man leadership for the Republican Party, one person for organization and another of equal status as party spokesman. Suggested Ray C. Bliss, Ohio GOP State Chairman since 1948 for organization post and a man like ex-Representative Walter H. Judd of Minnesota for spokesman post.

1965

April 30　　Supported President Johnson's sending of marines into the Dominican Republic to stabilize the situation.

August 17　　Stated at a press conference in Washington that he considered the Los Angeles riots a sympton of increasing nationwide lawlessness.

September 22　Stated in an interview at Gettysburg, Pennsylvania that French President Charles de Gaulle's initiation to end NATO's integrated military command would leave each nation with its own independent defense forces, meaning that defense through coalition does not work.

October 5　　Met with President Johnson in a secret conference discussing Presidential illness and ways of disclosing information about it to the public.

October 14　　Published *Waging Peace: The White House Years, 1956-1961.*

November 9　　Hospitalized with chest pains at Fort Gordon Army Hospital near Augusta, Georgia. Diagnosed as definite heart attack on November 12.

1966

January 31　　Supported President Johnson's decision to resume air attacks on North Vietnam.

March 9　　French Government formally announced its intention to withdraw all its armed forces from the North Atlantic Treaty Organization's integrated military command. It simultaneously announced that all NATO commands and installations on French territory had to either come under French military authority or leave French soil. France was not withdrawing from the North Atlantic Alliance.

March 22   Published an article in *Reader's Digest* condemning the draft card burners who had indicated their opposition to the war in Vietnam.

June 15   Endorsed Ronald Reagan, Republican candidate for Governor of California, when Reagan visited Eisenhower at his home in Gettysburg, Pennsylvania.

September 30   Told newspapermen in Chicago that he was in favor of using as much force as possible to win the war in Vietnam. He could not make recommendations because he did not know all the political considerations.

November 5   Defended former Vice President Richard M. Nixon against charges of President Johnson that Nixon was confusing the Allied position in regard to the United States pledge to withdraw troops from Vietnam if North Vietnam withdrew its forces. Eisenhower claimed that Nixon was the "best informed, most capable and most industrious Vice President in the history of the United States."

November 17   Visited President Johnson in the hospital following surgery upon the latter on November 16. President Johnson suggested the possibility of Eisenhower taking a trip to Asia and other parts of the world during or after the Spring of 1967.

December 12   Eisenhower underwent surgery for removal of his gall bladder at Walter Reed Army Medical Center. President Johnson visited him on December 16 and consulted with him on several issues.

1967

February 3   Issued statement that the Consular Convention between the United States and the Soviet Union was in the national interest and would "not impair our national security."

April 29   General William C. Westmoreland, Commander of United States forces in Vietnam visited Eisenhower in Palm Springs, California. Eisenhower later praised the United States' role in the war and the soldiers who served there.

June 9   Published *At Ease: Stories I Tell to Friends.* Reminiscences of the General's career.

August 5   Endorsed extension of bombing in North Vietnam saying that military targets should be bombed. He thought it would not enlarge the risk of China entering the war.

October 13   Supported the Administration's policy in Vietnam at a press conference on the eve of his 77th birthday. He deplored dissension in the United States, indicating that everyone wanted peace, but there had to be an honorable one.

October 25   The Citizens Committee for Peace with Freedom in Vietnam, of which Former Presidents Eisenhower and Truman were members, issued a statement expressing strong support for current United States policy in Vietnam.

November 28   Appeared on CBS-TV advocating a limited United States invasion of North Vietnam to eliminate the dangerous enemy artillery positions near the demilitarized zone separating North from South Vietnam. Eisenhower also indicated that the United States should pursue retreating enemy forces into Cambodia or Laos. Interview taped November 24.

November 29   White House announced donation of ex-President and Mrs. Dwight D. Eisenhower of their 230-acre home near Gettysburg, Pennsylvania, as an historic site on November 27. The property adjoins the Gettysburg National Military Park. Not open to the public during the Eisenhowers' lifetime.

November 30   Former Vice President Richard M. Nixon announced the engagement of his younger daughter Julie, 19, to David Eisenhower, 19, Eisenhower's grandson.

December 22   Urged the public to continue to support the war effort in Vietnam, indicating that world peace and even the fate of Southeast Asia was involved in the war.

1968

February 18   President Johnson visited Eisenhower at Palm Desert, California. Special Presidential Assistant Walt Rostow briefed the former President on the Vietnamese war.

March 31   President Johnson announced in a nationwide television address that he would not seek or accept nomination for another term as President. Also announced that he had unilaterally ordered a halt to all air and naval bombardments of North Vietnam except where every buildup threatened Allied positions. He called for reciprocal action by Hanoi along with the beginning of peace talks.

April 7   General Westmoreland visited Eisenhower at Eldorado, California, and briefed him on the war.

April 18   President Johnson visited Eisenhower in California to brief him on Honolulu talks as well as other military and diplomatic developments concerning Vietnam.

April 20   Eisenhower became ill and was flown to March Air Force Base Hospital in California. Hospital officials reported on April 30 that he had suffered a mild coronary—his fourth heart attack. He left the Base on May 14 and was transferred to Walter Reed Army Hospital.

June 5   Senator Robert F. Kennedy of New York, candidate for the Democratic Presidential nomination was shot. He died from the assassin's bullet on June 6.

June 11   President Johnson visited Eisenhower at Walter Reed Hospital.

June 16   Eisenhower suffered his fifth heart attack while recuperating at Walter Reed Army Medical Center.

July 18   Endorsed Richard M. Nixon for the Republican Presidential nomination at Walter Reed Hospital.

August 5-8   Republican National Convention at Miami Beach, Florida, nominated Richard M. Nixon for President and Governor Spiro T. Agnew of Maryland for Vice President.

August 5   Eisenhower addressed the Republican National Convention by closed-circuit television from Walter Reed Army Medical Center, emphasizing the dangers of Communism.

August 6   Suffered a sixth heart attack about ten hours after addressing the Republican Convention.

August 16   Suffered a seventh heart attack.

August 26-29   Democratic National Convention at Chicago, Illinois, nominated Vice President Hubert H. Humphrey for President and Senator Edmund S. Muskie of Maine for Vice President.

October 13-20   Salute to Eisenhower Week.

October 21   Eisenhower, in a *Reader's Digest* article, rebutted the view that he relied too much on his staff during his administration.

November 5   National elections. Richard M. Nixon elected President. Nixon received 31,770,237 votes winning 301 electoral votes. Vice President Humphrey received 31,270,533 votes winning 191 electoral votes. Governor George C. Wallace of Alabama received 9,906,149 votes winning 46 electoral votes.

November 6   President-elect Nixon visited Eisenhower at Walter Reed Hospital.

November 16   Eisenhower's granddaughter, Anne, married F. Echavarria-Uribe.

December 18   Brother, Earl Eisenhower, died.

December 22   Eisenhower's grandson David Eisenhower married Julie Nixon, daughter of President-elect Nixon.

1969

February 23   Eisenhower underwent an emergency operation to remove an acute obstruction of the intestine.

March 15   Suffered an episode of congestive heart failure—a condition in which the heart's pumping action becomes inadequate for the body's total needs.

March 28   Died at Walter Reed Army Medical Center at 12:25 P.M.

April 2   Buried at the Eisenhower Library, Abilene, Kansas.

DOCUMENTS

FIRST INAUGURAL ADDRESS
January 20, 1953

President Eisenhower urged the unity of all free peoples to strengthen the Free World. In order to further world peace the United States should be guided by certain fixed principles: (1) to develop sufficient defensive strength to deter aggression and promote world peace; (2) avoidance of appeasement in negotiations; (3) In order to maintain a position of strength, all free citizens must place the cause of national unity above their comfort; (4) never to use strength to impress American institutions on others; (5) determination to aid other nations in their search for freedom; (6) to encourage productivity and profitable trade in order to foster economic health; (7) to strengthen various regional relationships within the United Nations; (8) rejection of any idea of racial inferiority; (9) to strive to make the United Nations an effective force.

MY FRIENDS, before I begin the expression of those thoughts that I deem appropriate to this moment, would you permit me the privilege of uttering a little private prayer of my own. And I ask that you bow your heads:

Almighty God, as we stand here at this moment my future associates in the Executive branch of Government join me in beseeching that Thou will make full and complete our dedication to the service of the people in this throng, and their fellow citizens everywhere.

Give us, we pray, the power to discern clearly right from wrong, and allow all our words and actions to be governed thereby, and by the laws of this land. Especially we pray that our concern shall be for all the people regardless of station, race or calling.

May cooperation be permitted and be the mutual aim of those who, under the concepts of our Constitution, hold to differing political faiths; so that all may work for the good of our beloved country and Thy glory. Amen.

My fellow citizens:

The world and we have passed the midway point of a century of continuing challenge. We sense with all our faculties that forces of good and evil are massed and armed and opposed as rarely before in history.

This fact defines the meaning of this day. We are summoned by this honored and historic ceremony to witness more than the act of one citizen swearing his oath of service, in the presence of God. We are called as a people to give testimony in the sight of the world to our faith that the future shall belong to the free.

Since this century's beginning, a time of tempest has seemed to come upon the continents of the earth. Masses of Asia have awakened to strike off shackles of the past. Great nations of Europe have fought their bloodiest wars. Thrones have toppled and their vast empires have disappeared. New nations have been born.

For our own country, it has been a time of recurring trial. We have grown in power and in responsibility. We have passed through the anxieties of depression and of war to a summit unmatched in man's history. Seeking to secure peace in the world, we have had to fight through the forests of the Argonne to the shores of Iwo Jima, and to the cold mountains of Korea.

In the swift rush of great events, we find ourselves groping to know the full sense and meaning of these times in which we live. In our quest of understanding, we beseech God's guidance. We summon all our knowledge of the past and we scan all signs of the future. We bring all our wit and all our will to meet the question:

How far have we come in man's long pilgrimage from darkness toward the light? Are we nearing the light—a day of freedom and of peace for all mankind? Or are the shadows of another night closing in upon us?

Great as are the preoccupations absorbing us at home, concerned as we are with matters that deeply affect our livelihood today and our vision of the future, each of these domestic problems is dwarfed by, and often even created by, this question that involves all humankind.

This trial comes at a moment when man's power to achieve good or to inflict evil surpasses the brightest hopes and the sharpest fears of all ages. We can turn rivers in their courses, level mountains to the plains. Oceans and land and sky are avenues for our colossal commerce. Disease diminishes and life lengthens.

Yet the promise of this life is imperiled by the very genius that has made it possible. Nations amass wealth. Labor sweats to create—and turns out devices to level not only mountains but also cities. Science seems ready to confer upon us, as its final gift, the power to erase human life from this planet.

At such a time in history, we who are free must proclaim anew our faith. This faith is the abiding creed of our fathers. It is our faith in the deathless dignity of man, governed by eternal moral and natural laws.

This faith defines our full view of life. It establishes, beyond debate, those gifts of the Creator that are man's inalienable rights, and that make all men equal in His sight.

In the light of this equality, we know that the virtues most cherished by free people—love of truth, pride of work, devotion to country—all are treasures equally precious in the lives of the most humble and of the most exalted. The men who mine coal and fire furnaces, and balance ledgers, and turn lathes, and pick cotton, and heal the sick and plant corn—all serve as proudly and as profitably for America as the statesmen who draft treaties and the legislators who enact laws.

This faith rules our whole way of life. It decrees that we, the people, elect leaders not to rule but to serve. It asserts that we have the right to choice of our own work and to the reward of our own toil. It inspires the initiative that makes our productivity the wonder of the world. And it warns that any man who seeks to deny equality among all his brothers betrays the spirit of the free and invites the mockery of the tyrant.

It is because we, all of us, hold to these principles that the political changes accomplished this day do not imply turbulence, upheaval or disorder. Rather this change expresses a purpose of strengthening our dedication and devotion to the precepts of our founding documents, a conscious renewal of faith in our country and in the watchfulness of a Divine Providence.

The enemies of this faith know no god but force, no devotion but its use. They tutor men in treason. They feed upon the hunger of others. Whatever defies them, they torture, especially the truth.

Here, then, is joined no argument between slightly differing philosophies. This conflict strikes directly at the faith of our fathers and the lives of our sons. No principle or treasure that we hold, from the spiritual knowledge of our free schools and churches to the creative magic of free labor and capital, nothing lies safely beyond the reach of this struggle.

Freedom is pitted against slavery; lightness against the dark.

The faith we hold belongs not to us alone but to the free of all the world. This common bond binds the grower of rice in Burma and the planter of wheat in Iowa, the shepherd in southern Italy and the mountaineer in the Andes. It confers a common dignity upon the French soldier who dies in Indo-China, the British soldier killed in Malaya, the American life given in Korea.

We know, beyond this, that we are linked to all free peoples not merely by a noble idea but by a simple need. No free people can for long cling to any privilege or enjoy any safety in economic solitude. For all our own material might, even we need markets in the world for the surpluses of our farms and our factories. Equally, we need for these same farms and factories vital materials and products of distant lands. This basic law of interdependence, so manifest in the commerce of peace, applies with thousand-fold intensity in the event of war.

So we are persuaded by necessity and by belief that the strength of all free peoples lies in unity; their danger, in discord.

To produce this unity, to meet the challenge of our time, destiny has laid upon our country the responsibility of the free world's leadership.

So it is proper that we assure our friends once again that, in the discharge of this responsibility, we Americans know and we observe the difference between world leadership and imperialism; between firmness and truculence; between a thoughtfully calculated goal and spasmodic reaction to the stimulus of emergencies.

We wish our friends the world over to know this above all: we face the threat—not with dread and confusion—but with confidence and conviction.

We feel this moral strength because we know that we are not helpless prisoners of history. We are free men. We shall remain free, never to be proven guilty of the one capital offense against freedom, a lack of stanch faith.

In pleading our just cause before the bar of history and in pressing our labor for world peace, we shall be guided by certain fixed principles. These principles are:

1. Abhorring war as a chosen way to balk the purposes of those who threaten us, we hold it to be the first task of statesmanship to develop the strength that will deter the forces of aggression and promote the conditions of peace. For, as it must be the supreme purpose of all free men, so it must be the dedication of their leaders, to save humanity from preying itself.

In the light of this principle, we stand ready to engage with any and all others in joint effort to remove the causes of mutual fear and distrust among nations, so as to make possible drastic reduction of armaments. The sole requisites for undertaking such effort are that—in their purpose—they be aimed logically and honestly toward secure peace for all; and that—in their result—they provide methods by which every participating nation will prove good faith in carrying out its pledge.

2. Realizing that common sense and common decency alike dictate the futility of appeasement, we shall never try to placate an aggressor by the false and wicked bargain of trading honor for security. Americans, indeed, all free men, remember that in the final choice a soldier's pack is not so heavy a burden as a prisoner's chains.

3. Knowing that only a United States that is strong and immensely productive can help defend freedom in our world, we view our Nation's strength and security as a trust upon which rests the hope of free men everywhere. It is the firm duty of each of our free citizens and of every free citizen everywhere to place the cause of his country before the comfort, the convenience of himself.

4. Honoring the identity and the special heritage of each nation in the world, we shall never use our strength to try to impress upon another people our own cherished political and economic institutions.

5. Assessing realistically the needs and capacities of proven friends of freedom, we shall strive to help them to achieve their own security and well-being. Likewise, we shall count upon them to assume, within the

limits of their resources, their full and just burdens in the common defense of freedom.

6. Recognizing economic health as an indispensable basis of military strength and the free world's peace, we shall strive to foster everywhere, and to practice ourselves, policies that encourage productivity and profitable trade. For the impoverishment of any single people in the world means danger to the well-being of all other peoples.

7. Appreciating that economic need, military security and political wisdom combine to suggest regional groupings of free peoples, we hope, within the framework of the United Nations, to help strengthen such special bonds the world over. The nature of these ties must vary with the different problems of different areas.

In the Western Hemisphere, we enthusiastically join with all our neighbors in the work of perfecting a community of fraternal trust and common purpose.

In Europe, we ask that enlightened and inspired leaders of the Western nations strive with renewed vigor to make the unity of their peoples a reality. Only as free Europe unitedly marshals its strength can it effectively safeguard, even with our help, its spiritual and cultural heritage.

8. Conceiving the defense of freedom, like freedom itself, to be one and indivisible, we hold all continents and peoples in equal regard and honor. We reject any insinuation that one race or another, one people or another, is in any sense inferior or expendable.

9. Respecting the United Nations as the living sign of all people's hope for peace, we shall strive to make it not merely an eloquent symbol but an effective force. And in our quest for an honorable peace, we shall neither compromise, nor tire, nor ever cease.

By these rules of conduct, we hope to be known to all peoples.

By their observance, an earth of peace may become not a vision but a fact.

This hope—this supreme aspiration—must rule the way we live.

We must be ready to dare all for our country. For history does not long entrust the care of freedom to the weak or the timid. We must acquire proficiency in defense and display stamina in purpose.

We must be willing, individually and as a Nation, to accept whatever sacrifices may be required of us. A people that values its privileges above its principles soon loses both.

These basic precepts are not lofty abstractions, far removed from matters of daily living. They are laws of spiritual strength that generate and define our material strength. Patriotism means equipped forces and a prepared citizenry. Moral stamina means more energy and more productivity, on the farm and in the factory. Love of liberty means the guarding of every resource that makes freedom possible—from the sanctity of our families and the wealth of our soil to the genious of our scientists.

And so each citizen plays an indispensable role. The productivity of our heads, our hands and our hearts is the source of all the strength we can command, for both the enrichment of our lives and the winning of the peace.

No person, no home, no community can be beyond the reach of this call. We are summoned to act in wisdom and in conscience, to work with industry, to teach with persuasion, to preach with conviction, to weigh our every deed with care and with compassion. For this truth must be clear before us: whatever America hopes to bring to pass in the world must first come to pass in the heart of America.

The peace we seek, then, is nothing less than the practice and fulfillment of our whole faith among ourselves and in our dealings with others. This signifies more than the stilling of guns, easing the sorrow of war. More than escape from death, it is a way of life. More than a haven for the weary, it is a hope for the brave.

This is the hope that beckons us onward in this century of trial. This is the work that awaits us all, to be done with bravery, with charity, and with prayer to Almighty God.

My citizens—I thank you.

FIRST ANNUAL MESSAGE
February 2, 1953

In this first policy statement to the Congress President Eisenhower outlined a major program of domestic and foreign changes to be made by the new Administration. Plans were indicated to meet American obligations abroad for the defense of the Free World and to develop a domestic policy which will aid all Americans.

Mr. President, Mr. Speaker, Members of the Eighty-Third Congress:

For the warmth of your reception my deep and grateful thanks.

I welcome the honor of appearing before you to deliver my first message to the Congress.

It is manifestly the joint purpose of the congressional leadership and of this administration to justify the summons to governmental responsibility issued last November by the American people.

The grand labors of this leadership will involve—

Application of America's influence in world affairs with such fortitude and such foresight that it will deter aggression and eventually secure peace;

Establishment of a national administration of such integrity and such efficiency that its honor at home will ensure respect abroad;

Encouragement of those incentives that inspire creative initiative in our economy, so that its productivity may fortify freedom everywhere; and

Dedication to the well-being of all our citizens and to the attainment of equality of opportunity for all, so that our Nation will ever act with the strength of unity in every task to which it is called. . . .

II

Our country has come through a painful period of trial and disillusionment since the victory of 1945. We anticipated a world of peace and cooperation. The calculated pressures of aggressive communism have forced us, instead, to live in a world of turmoil.

From this costly experience we have learned one clear lesson. We have learned that the free world cannot indefinitely remain in a posture of paralyzed tension. To do so leaves forever to the aggressor the choice of time and place and means to cause greatest hurt to us at least cost to himself.

This administration has, therefore, begun the definition of a new, positive foreign policy. This policy will be governed by certain basic ideas. They are these:

First. Our foreign policy must be clear, consistent, and confident. This means that it must be the product of genuine, continuous cooperation between the executive and the legislative branches of this Government. It must be developed and directed in the spirit of true bipartisanship. And I assure you, Members of this Congress, I mean that fully, earnestly, and sincerely.

Second. The policy we embrace must be a coherent global policy. The freedom we cherish and defend in Europe and in the Americas is no different from the freedom that is imperiled in Asia.

Third. Our policy, dedicated to making the free world secure, will envision all peaceful methods and devices—except breaking faith with our friends. We shall never acquiesce in the enslavement of any people in order to purchase fancied gain for ourselves. I shall ask the Congress at a later date to join in an appropriate resolution making clear that this Government recognizes no kind of commitment contained in secret understandings of the past with foreign governments which permit this kind of enslavement.

Fourth. The policy we pursue will recognize the truth that no single country, even one so powerful as ours, can alone defend the liberty of all nations threatened by Communist aggression from without or subversion within. Mutual security means effective mutual cooperation. For the United States, this means that, as a matter of common sense and national interest, we shall give help to other nations in the measure that they strive earnestly to do their full share of the common task. No wealth of aid could compensate for poverty of spirit. The heart of every free nation must be honestly dedicated to the preserving of its own independence and security.

Fifth. Our policy will be designed to foster the advent of practical unity in Western Europe. The nations of that region have contributed notably to the effort of sustaining the security of the free world. From the jungles of Indochina and Malaya to the northern shores of Europe, they have vastly improved their defensive strength. Where called upon to do so, they have made costly and bitter sacrifices to hold the line of freedom.

But the problem of security demands closer cooperation among the nations of Europe than has been known to date. Only a more closely integrated economic and political system can provide the greatly increased economic strength needed to maintain both necessary military readiness and respectable living standards. . . .

The needed unity of Western Europe manifestly cannot be manufactured from without; it can only be created from within. But it is right and necessary that we encourage Europe's leaders by informing them of the high value we place upon the earnestness of their efforts toward this goal. Real progress will be conclusive evidence to the American people that our material sacrifices in the cause of collective security are matched by essential political, economic, and military accomplishments in Western Europe.

Sixth. Our foreign policy will recognize the importance of profitable and equitable world trade.

A substantial beginning can and should be made by our friends themselves. Europe, for example, is now marked by checkered areas of labor surplus and labor shortage, of agricultural areas needing machines and industrial areas needing food. Here and elsewhere we can hope that our friends will take the initiative in creating broader markets and more dependable currencies, to allow greater exchange of goods and services among themselves.

Action along these lines can create an economic environment that will invite vital help from us.

Such help includes—

First, revising our customs regulations to remove procedural obstacles to profitable trade. I further recommend that the Congress take the Reciprocal Trade Agreements Act under immediate study and extend it by appropriate legislation. This objective must not ignore legitimate safeguarding of domestic industries, agriculture, and labor standards. In all executive study and recommendations on this problem labor and management and farmers alike will be earnestly consulted.

Second, doing whatever our Government can properly do to encourage the flow of ᐳprivate American investment abroad. This involves, as a serious and explicit purpose of our foreign policy, the encouragement of a hospitable climate for such investment in foreign nations.

Third, availing ourselves of facilities overseas for the economical production of manufactured articles which are needed for mutual defense and which are not seriously competitive with our own normal peacetime production.

Fourth, receiving from the rest of the world, in equitable exchange for what we supply, greater amounts of important raw materials which we do not ourselves possess in adequate quantities.

III

In this general discussion of our foreign policy, I must make special mention of the war in Korea.

This war is, for Americans, the most painful phase of Communist aggression throughout the world. It is clearly a part of the same calculated assault that the aggressor is simultaneously pressing in Indochina and in Malaya, and of the strategic situation that manifestly embraces the island of Formosa and the Chinese Nationalist forces there. The working out of any military solution to the Korean war will inevitably affect all these areas.

The administration is giving immediate increased attention to the development of additional Republic of Korea forces. The citizens of that country have proved their capacity as fighting men and their eagerness to take a greater share in the defense of their homeland. Organization, equipment, and training will allow them to do so. Increased assistance to Korea for this purpose conforms fully to our global policies.

In June 1950, following the aggressive attack on the Republic of Korea, the United States Seventh Fleet was instructed both to prevent attack upon Formosa and also to insure that Formosa should not be used as a base of operations against the Chinese Communist mainland.

This has meant, in effect, that the United States Navy was required to serve as a defensive arm of Communist China. Regardless of the situation in 1950, since the date of that order the Chinese Communists have invaded Korea to attack the United Nations forces there. They have consistently rejected the proposals of the United Nations Command for armistice. They recently joined with Soviet Russia in rejecting the armistice proposal sponsored in the United Nations by the Government of India. This proposal had been accepted by the United States and 53 other nations.

Consequently there is no longer any logic or sense in a condition that required the United States Navy to assume defensive responsibilities on behalf of the Chinese Communists. This permitted those Communists, with greater impunity, to kill our soldiers and those of our United Nations allies in Korea.

I am, therefore, issuing instructions that the Seventh Fleet no longer be employed to shield Communist China. Permit me to make crystal clear, this order implies no aggressive intent on our part. But we certainly have no obligation to protect a nation fighting us in Korea.

IV

Our labor for peace in Korea and in the world imperatively demands the maintenance by the United States of a strong fighting service ready for any contingency.

Our problem is to achieve adequate military strength within the limits of endurable strain upon our economy. To amass military power without regard to our economic capacity would be to defend ourselves against one kind of disaster by inviting another.

Both military and economic objectives demand a single national military policy, proper coordination of our armed services, and effective consolidation of certain logistics functions.

We must eliminate waste and duplication of effort in the armed services.

We must realize clearly that size alone is not sufficient. The biggest force is not necessarily the best force—we want the best.

We must not let traditions or habits of the past stand in the way of developing an efficient military force. All members of our forces must be ever mindful that they serve under a single flag and for a single cause.

We must effectively integrate our armament programs and plan them in such careful relation to our industrial facilities that we assure the best use of our manpower and our materials. . . .

The statutory function of the National Security Council is to assist the President in the formulation and coordination of significant domestic, foreign, and military policies required for the security of this Nation. In these days of tension it is essential that this central body have the vitality to perform effectively its statutory role. I propose to see that it does so.

Careful formulation of policies must be followed by clear understanding of them by all peoples. A related need, therefore, is to make more effective all activities of the Government related to international information. . . .

A unified and dynamic effort in this whole field is essential to the security of the United States and of the other peoples in the community of free nations. There is but one sure way to avoid global war—and that is to win the cold war.

While retaliatory power is one strong deterrent to a would-be aggressor, another powerful deterrent is defensive power. No enemy is likely to attempt an attack foredoomed to failure.

Because the building of a completely impenetrable defense against attack is still not possible, total defensive strength must include civil defense preparedness. Because we have incontrovertible evidence that Soviet Russia possesses atomic weapons, this kind of protection becomes sheer necessity.

Civil defense responsibilities primarily belong to the State and local governments, including recruiting, training, and organizing volunteers to meet any emergency. The immediate job of the Federal Government is to provide leadership, to supply technical guidance, and to continue to strengthen its civil defense stockpile of medical, engineering, and related supplies and equipment. This work must go forward without lag.

V

I have referred to the inescapable need for economic health and strength if we are to maintain adequate military power and exert influential leadership for peace in the world.

Our immediate task is to chart a fiscal and economic policy that can:

First, reduce the planned deficits and then balance the budget, which means, among other things, reducing Federal expenditures to the safe minimum;

Second, meet the huge costs of our defense;

Third, properly handle the burden of our inheritance of debt and obligations;

Fourth, check the menace of inflation;

Fifth, work toward the earliest possible reduction of the tax burden;

Sixth, make constructive plans to encourage the initiative of our citizens.

It is important that all of us understand that this administration does not and cannot begin its task with a clean slate. Much already has been written on the record, beyond our power quickly to erase or to amend. This record includes our inherited burden of indebtedness and obligations and deficits. . . .

The present authorized Government-debt limit is 275 billion dollars. The forecast presented by the outgoing administration with the fiscal year 1954 budget indicates that—before the end of the fiscal year and at the peak of demand for payments during that year—the total Government debt may approach and even exceed that limit. Unless budgeted deficits are checked, the momentum of past programs will force an increase of the statutory debt limit.

Permit me this one understatement: To meet and to correct this situation will not be easy.

Permit me this one assurance: Every department head and I are determined to do everything we can to resolve it.

The first order of business is the elimination of the annual deficit. This cannot be achieved merely be exhortation. It demands the concerted action of all those in responsible positions in the Government and the earnest cooperation of the Congress. . . .

Getting control of the budget requires also that State and local governments and interested groups of citizens restrain themselves in their demands upon the Congress.

A balanced budget is an essential first measure in checking further depreciation in the buying power of the dollar. This is one of the critical steps to be taken to bring an end to planned inflation. Our purpose is to manage the Government's finances so as to help and not hinder each family in balancing its own budget.

Reduction of taxes will be justified only as we show we can succeed in bringing the budget under control. As the budget is balanced and inflation checked, the tax burden that today stifles initiative can and must be eased.

Until we can determine the extent to which expenditures can be reduced, it would not be wise to reduce our revenues.

Meanwhile, the tax structure as a whole demands review. . . . Clarification and simplification in the tax laws as well as the regulations will be undertaken.

In the entire area of fiscal policy—which must, in its various aspects, be treated in recommendations to the Congress in coming weeks—there can now be stated certain basic facts and principles.

First. It is axiomatic that our economy is a highly complex and sensitive mechanism. Hasty and ill-considered action of any kind could seriously upset the subtle equation that encompasses debts, obligations, expenditures, defense demands, deficits, taxes, and the general economic health of the Nation. Our goals can be clear, our start toward them can be immediate—but action must be gradual.

Second. It is clear that too great a part of the national debt comes due in too short a time. The Department of the Treasury will undertake—indeed has undertaken—at suitable times a program of extending part of the debt over longer periods and gradually placing greater amounts in the hands of longer-term investors.

Third. Past differences in policy between the Treasury and the Federal Reserve Board have helped to encourage inflation. Henceforth, I expect that their single purpose shall be to serve the whole Nation by policies designed to stabilize the economy and encourage the free play of our people's genius for individual initiative.

In encouraging this initiative, no single item in our current problems has received more thoughtful consideration by my associates, and by the many individuals called into our counsels, than the matter of price and wage control by law.

The great economic strength of our democracy has developed in an atmosphere of freedom. The character of our people resists artificial and arbitrary controls of any kind. Direct controls, except those on credit, deal not with the real causes of inflation but only with its symptoms. In times of national emergency, this kind of control has a role to play. Our whole system, however, is based upon the assumption that, normally, we should combat wide fluctuations in our price structure by relying largely on the effective use of sound fiscal and monetary policy, and upon the natural workings of economic law.

Moreover, American labor and American business can best resolve their wage problems across the bargaining table. Government should refrain from sitting in with them unless, in extreme cases, the public welfare requires protection.

We are, of course, living in an international situation that is neither an emergency demanding full mobilization, nor is it peace. No one can know how long this condition will persist. Consequently, we are forced to learn many new things as we go along—clinging to what works, discarding what does not. . . .

Accordingly, I do not intend to ask for a renewal of the present wage and price controls on April 30, 1953. In the meantime, steps will be taken to eliminate controls in an orderly manner, and to terminate special agencies no longer needed for this purpose. It is obviously to be expected that the removal of these controls will result in individual price changes—some will move up, some down. But a maximum of freedom in market prices as well as in collective bargaining is characteristic of a truly free people.

I believe also that material and product controls should be ended, except with respect to defense priorities and scarce and critical items essential for our defense. I shall recommend to the Congress that legislation be enacted to continue authority for such remaining controls of this type as will be necessary after the expiration of the existing statute on June 30, 1953.

I recommend the continuance of the authority for Federal control over rents in those communities in which serious housing shortages exist. These are chiefly the so-called defense areas. In these and all areas the Federal Government should withdraw from the control of rents as soon as practicable. But before they are removed entirely, each legislature should have full opportunity to take over, within its own State, responsibility for this function.

It would be idle to pretend that all our problems in this whole field of prices will solve themselves by mere Federal withdrawal from direct controls.

We shall have to watch trends closely. If the freer functioning of our economic system, as well as the indirect controls which can be appropriately employed, prove insufficient during this period of strain and tension, I shall promptly ask this Congress to enact such legislation as may be required.

In facing all these problems—wages, prices, production, tax rates, fiscal policy, deficits—everywhere we remain constantly mindful that the time for sacrifice has not ended. But we are concerned with the encouragement of competitive enterprise and individual initiative precisely because we know them to be our Nation's abiding sources of strength.

VI

Our vast world responsibility accents with urgency our people's elemental right to a government whose clear qualities are loyalty, security, efficiency, economy, and integrity.

The safety of America and the trust of the people alike demand that the personnel of the Federal Government be loyal in their motives and reliable in the discharge of their duties. Only a combination of both loyalty and reliability promises genuine security.

To state this principle is easy; to apply it can be difficult. But this security we must and we shall have. By way of example, all principal new appointees to departments and agencies have been investigated at their own request by the Federal Bureau of Investigation.

Confident of your understanding and cooperation, I know that the primary responsibility for keeping out the disloyal and the dangerous rests squarely upon the executive branch. When this branch so conducts itself as to require policing by another branch of the Government, it invites its own disorder and confusion.

I am determined to meet this responsibility of the Executive. The heads of all executive departments and agencies have been instructed to initiate at once effective programs of security with respect to their personnel. . . .

Our people, of course, deserve and demand of their Federal Government more than security of personnel. They demand, also, efficient and logical organization, true to constitutional principles. . . .

There is more involved here than realining the wheels and smoothing the gears of administrative machinery. The Congress rightfully expects the Executive to take the initiative in discovering and removing outmoded functions and eliminating duplication.

One agency, for example, whose head has promised early and vigorous action to provide greater efficiency is the Post Office. One of the oldest institutions of our Federal Government, its service should be the best. Its employees should merit and receive the high regard and esteem of the citizens of the Nation. There are today in some areas of the postal service, both waste and incompetence to be corrected. With cooperation of the Congress, and taking advantage of its accumulated experience in postal affairs, the Postmaster General will institute a program directed at improving service while at the same time reducing costs and decreasing deficits.

In all departments, dedication to these basic precepts of security and efficiency, integrity, and economy can and will produce an administration deserving of the trust the people have placed in it.

Our people have demanded nothing less than good, efficient government. They shall get nothing less. . . .

Another of its major concerns is our country's island possessions. Here, one matter deserves attention. The platforms of both political parties promised immediate statehood to Hawaii. The people of that Territory have earned that status. Statehood should be granted promptly with the first election scheduled for 1954. . . .

IX

The determination of labor policy must be governed not by the vagaries of political expediency but by the firmest principles and convictions. Slanted partisan appeals to American workers, spoken as if they were a group apart, necessitating a special language and treatment, are an affront to the fullness of their dignity as American citizens.

The truth in matters of labor policy has become obscured in controversy. The very meaning of economic freedom as it affects labor has become confused. This misunderstanding has provided a climate of opinion favoring the growth of governmental paternalism in labor relations. This tendency, if left uncorrected, could end only by producing a bureaucratic despotism. Economic freedom is, in fact, the requisite of greater prosperity for every American who earns his own living.

In the field of labor legislation, only a law that merits the respect and support of both labor and management can help reduce the loss of wages and of production through strikes and stoppages, and thus add to the total economic strength of the Nation. . . .

Government can do a great deal to aid the settlement of labor disputes without allowing itself to be employed as an ally of either side. Its proper role in industrial strife is to encourage the processes of mediation and conciliation. These processes can successfully be directed only by a government free from the taint of any suspicion that it is partial or punitive.

X

Our civil and social rights form a central part of the heritage we are striving to defend on all fronts and with all our strength.

I believe with all my heart that our vigilant guarding of these rights is a sacred obligation binding upon every citizen. To be true to one's own freedom is, in essence, to honor and respect the freedom of all others.

A cardinal ideal in this heritage we cherish is the equality of rights of all citizens of every race and color and creed.

We know that discrimination against minorities persists despite our allegiance to this ideal. Such discrimination—confined to no one section of the Nation—is but the outward testimony to the persistence of distrust and of fear in the hearts of men.

This fact makes all the more vital the fighting of these wrongs by each individual, in every station of life, in his every deed.

Much of the answer lies in the power of fact, fully publicized; of persuasion, honestly pressed; and of conscience, justly aroused. These are methods familiar to our way of life, tested and proven wise.

I propose to use whatever authority exists in the office of the President to end segregation in the District of Columbia, including the Federal Government, and any segregation in the Armed Forces. . . .

There is one sphere in which civil rights are inevitably involved in Federal legislation. This is the sphere of immigration.

It is a manifest right of our Government to limit the number of immigrants our Nation can absorb. It is also a manifest right of our Government to set reasonable requirements on the character and the numbers of the people who come to share our land and our freedom. . . .

Existing legislation contains injustices. It does, in fact, discriminate. I am informed by Members of the Congress that it was realized, at the time of its enactment, that future study of the proper basis of determining quotas would be necessary.

I am therefore requesting the Congress to review this legislation and to enact a statute which will at one and the same time guard our legitimate national interests and be faithful to our basic ideas of freedom and fairness to all.

In another but related area—that of social rights—we see most clearly the new application of old ideas of freedom.

This administration is profoundly aware of two great needs born of our living in a complex industrial economy. First, the individual citizen must have safeguards against personal disaster inflicted by forces beyond his control; second, the welfare of the people demands effective and economical performance by the Government of certain indispensable social services.

In the light of this responsibility, certain general purposes and certain concrete measures are plainly indicated now.

There is urgent need for greater effectiveness in our programs, both public and private, offering safeguards against the privations that too often come with unemployment, old age, illness, and accident. The provisions of the old-age and survivors insurance law should promptly be extended to cover millions of citizens who have been left out of the social-security system. No less important is the encouragement of privately sponsored pension plans. Most important of all, of course, is renewed effort to check the inflation which destroys so much of the value of all social-security payments.

Our school system demands some prompt, effective help. During each of the last 2 years, more than 1½ million children have swelled the elementary and secondary school population of the country. Generally, the school population is proportionately higher in States with low per capita income. This whole situation calls for careful congressional study and action. I am sure you share my conviction that the firm conditions of Federal aid must be proved need and proved lack of local income.

One phase of the school problem demands special attention. The school population of many districts has been greatly increased by the swift growth of defense activities. These activities have added little or nothing to the tax resources of the communities affected. Legislation aiding construction of schools in these districts expires on June 20. This law should be renewed; and, likewise, the partial payments for current operating expenses for these particular school districts should be made, including the deficiency requirement of the current fiscal year.

Public interest similarly demands one prompt specific action in protection of the general consumer. The Food and Drug Administration should be authorized to continue its established and necessary program of factory inspections. The invalidation of these inspections by the Supreme Court of December 8, 1952, was based solely on the fact that the present law contains inconsistent and unclear provisions. These should be promptly corrected.

I am well aware that beyond these few immediate measures there remains much to be done. The health and housing needs of our people call for intelligently planned programs. Involved are the solvency of the whole security system; and its guarding against exploitation by the irresponsible.

To bring clear purpose and orderly procedure into this field, I anticipate a thorough study of the proper relationship among Federal, State, and local programs. I shall shortly send you specific recommendations for establishing an appropriate commission, together with a reorganization plan defining new administrative status for all Federal activities in health, education, and social security.

I repeat that there are many important subjects of which I make no mention today. Among these is our great and growing body of veterans. America has traditionally been generous in caring for the disabled—and the widow and the orphan of the fallen. These millions remain close to all our hearts. Proper care of our uniformed citizens and appreciation of the past service of our veterans are part of our accepted governmental responsibilities.

XI

We have surveyed briefly some problems of our people and a portion of the tasks before us.

The hope of freedom itself depends in real measure upon our strength, our heart, and our wisdom.

We must be strong in arms. We must be strong in the source of all our armament, our productivity. We all—workers and farmers, foremen and financiers, technicians and builders—all must produce, produce more, and produce yet more.

We must be strong, above all, in the spiritual resources upon which all else depends. We must be devoted with all our heart to the values we defend. We must know that each of these values and virtues applies with equal force at the ends of the earth and in our relations with our neighbor next door. We must know that freedom expresses itself with equal eloquence in the right of workers to strike in the nearby factory, and in the yearnings and sufferings of the peoples of Eastern Europe.

As our heart summons our strength, our wisdom must direct it.

There is, in world affairs, a steady course to be followed between an assertion of strength that is truculent and a confession of helplessness that is cowardly.

There is, in our affairs at home, a middle way between untrammeled freedom of the individual and the demands for the welfare of the whole Nation. This way must avoid government by bureaucracy as carefully as it avoids neglect of the helpless.

In every area of political action, free men must think before they can expect to win. . . .

THE PRESIDENT'S NEWS CONFERENCE
February 25, 1953

In this News Conference the President stated that within reason he would go almost anywhere to meet anybody in order to foster world peace.

Q. Robert E. Clark, International News Service:

Stalin is quoted a few weeks ago as saying that he would look favorably on a face to face meeting with you. Do you think anything would be accomplished by such a meeting at this time? Would you be willing to go out of this country to meet with Stalin?

The President:

Well, you are asking me in advance either to say I think there is a good chance, or isn't a good chance.

I will say this: I would meet anybody, anywhere, where I thought there was the slightest chance of doing any good, as long as it was in keeping with what the American people expect of their chief executive. In other words, I wouldn't want to just say, "Yes, I will go anywhere." I would go to any suitable spot, let's say halfway between, and talk with anybody, and with the full knowledge of our allies and friends as to the kind of thing I was talking about, because this business of defending freedom is a big job. It is not just one nation's job. . . .

SPECIAL MESSAGE TO CONGRESS
REORGANIZATION PLAN 1 OF 1953 CREATING THE
DEPARTMENT OF HEALTH, EDUCATION, AND WELFARE
March 12, 1953

President Eisenhower urged the creation of this new Cabinet post to help improve the administration of the vital health, education, and social security functions. He traces the history of efforts to create such a department and then indicates the departmental structure to be established.

March 12, 1953

To the Congress of the United States:

I transmit herewith Reorganization Plan No. 1 of 1953, prepared in accordance with the provisions of the Reorganization Act of 1949, as amended.

In my message of February 2, 1953, I stated that I would send to the Congress a reorganization plan defining a new administrative status for Federal activities in health, education, and social security. This plan carries out that intention by creating a Department of Health, Education, and Welfare as one of the executive departments of the Government and by transferring to it the various units of the Federal Security Agency. The Department will be headed by a Secretary of Health, Education, and Welfare, who will be assisted by an Under Secretary and two Assistant Secretaries.

The purpose of this plan is to improve the administration of the vital health, education, and social security functions now being carried on in the Federal Security Agency by giving them departmental rank. Such action is demanded by the importance and magnitude of these functions, which affect the well-being of millions of our citizens. The programs carried on by the Public Health Service include, for example, the conduct and promotion of research into the prevention and cure of such dangerous ailments as cancer and heart disease. The Public Health Service also administers payments to the States for the support of their health services and for urgently needed hospital construction. The Office of Education collects, analyzes and distributes to school administrators throughout the country information relating to the organization and management of educational systems. Among its other functions is the provision of financial help to school districts burdened by activities of the United States Government. State assistance to the aged, the blind, the totally disabled, and dependent children is heavily supported by grants-in-aid administered through the Social Security Administration. The old age and survivors insurance system and child development and welfare programs are additional responsibilities of that Administration. Other offices of the Federal Security Agency are responsible for the conduct of Federal vocational rehabilitation programs and for the enforcement of food and drug laws.

There should be an unremitting effort to improve those health, education, and social security programs which have proved their value. I have already recommended the expansion of the social security system to cover persons not now protected, the continuation of assistance to school districts whose population has been greatly increased by the expansion of defense activities, and the strengthening of our food and drug laws.

But good intent and high purpose are not enough; all such programs depend for their success upon efficient, responsible administration. I have recently taken action to assure that the Federal Security Administrator's views are given proper consideration in executive councils by inviting her to attend meetings of the Cabinet. Now the establishment of the new Department provided for in Reorganization Plan No. 1 of 1953 will give the needed additional assurance that these matters will receive the full consideration they deserve in the whole operation of the Government. . . .

The present plan will make it possible to give the officials directing the Department titles indicative of their responsibilities and salaries comparable to those received by their counterparts in other executive departments. The plan opens the way to further administrative improvement by authorizing the Secretary to centralize services and activities common to the several agencies of the Department. It also establishes a uniform method of appointment for the heads of the three major constituent agencies. At present, the Surgeon General and the Commissioner of Education are appointed by the President and confirmed by the Senate, while the Commissioner for Social Security is appointed by the Federal Security Administrator. Hereafter, all three will be Presidential appointees subject to Senate confirmation.

I believe, and this plan reflects my conviction, that these several fields of Federal activity should continue within the framework of a single department. The plan at the same time assures that the Office of Education and the Public Health Service retain the professional and substantive responsibilities vested by law in those agencies or in their heads. The Surgeon General, the Commissioner of Education and the Commissioner of Social Security will all have direct access to the Secretary.

There should be in the Department an Advisory Committee on Education, made up of persons chosen by the Secretary from outside the Federal Government, which would advise the Secretary with respect to the educational programs of the Department. The creation of such a Committee as an advisory body to the Secretary will help ensure the maintenance of responsibility for the public educational system in State and local governments while preserving the national interest in education through appropriate Federal action.

RADIO AND TELEVISION ADDRESS
TO THE AMERICAN PEOPLE
ANNOUNCEMENT OF SIGNING OF KOREAN ARMISTICE
July 26, 1953

President Eisenhower announced the signing of the armistice and further indicated that the United States intended to help develop the economic stability of the Republic of Korea.

My fellow citizens:

Tonight we greet, with prayers of thanksgiving, the official news that an armistice was signed almost an hour ago in Korea. It will quickly bring to an end the fighting between the United Nations forces and the Communist armies. For this Nation the cost of repelling aggression has been high. In thousands of homes it has been incalculable. It has been paid in terms of tragedy.

With special feelings of sorrow—and of solemn gratitude—we think of those who were called upon to lay down their lives in that far-off land to prove once again that only courage and sacrifice can keep freedom alive upon the earth. To the widows and orphans of this war, and to those veterans who bear disabling wounds, America renews tonight her pledge of lasting devotion and care.

Our thoughts turn also to those other Americans wearied by many months of imprisonment behind the enemy lines. The swift return of all of them will bring joy to thousands of families. It will be evidence of good faith on the part of those with whom we have signed this armistice.

Soldiers, sailors, and airmen of 16 different countries have stood as partners beside us throughout these long and bitter months. America's thanks go to each. In this struggle we have seen the United Nations meet the challenge of aggression—not with pathetic words of protest, but with deeds of decisive purpose. It is proper that we salute particularly the valorous armies of the Republic of Korea, for they have done even more than prove their right to freedom. Inspired by President Syngman Rhee, they have given an example of courage and patriotism which again demonstrtes that men of the West and men of the East can fight and work and live together side by side in pursuit of a just and noble cause.

And so at long last the carnage of war is to cease and the negotiations of the conference table is to begin. On this Sabbath evening each of us devoutly prays that all nations may come to see the wisdom of composing differences in this fashion before, rather than after, there is resort to brutal and futile battle.

Now as we strive to bring about that wisdom, there is, in this moment of sober satisfaction, one thought that must discipline our emotions and steady our resolution. It is this: we have won an armistice on a single battleground —not peace in the world. We may not now relax our guard nor cease our quest.

Throughout the coming months, during the period of prisoner screening and exchange, and during the possibly longer period taken in Korea more than three months ago. The completed survey has been reviewed by the National Security Council. On the basis of its analysis and recommendation, I am convinced that the security interests of the United States clearly indicate the need to act promptly not only to meet immediate relief needs but also to begin the long-range work of restoring the Korean economy to health and strength.

While this program is geared to meeting simply indispensable needs, its precise shape in the future must to some extent be governed by future events. It must take account of the fact that our objectives in Korea are not completely attained so long as Korea remains divided; and the assistance now proposed is carefully designed to avoid projects which would prove valueless in a united country. The implementation of the program will depend upon the continued cooperation of the Government of the Republic of Korea with the United States and the United Nations Command.

There is, as I have said, a second fact beyond the desperate need of Korea which, I believe, must govern our action at this time. It is the chance—and the need—for the free peoples to give clear and tangible testimony to their awareness that true peace means more than the simple absence of war. It means moral and material health. It means political order and economic progress. It means the living hope, in the hearts of all peoples, that tomorrow can bring a more just, a more free, a more productive life than today.

No people on earth has proved more valiantly than the people of Korea their right to hold and cherish this hope. Ours is the task to help and nourish this hope—for the sake of one brave people, and for the sake of all peoples who wait and watch to see if free men can be as wise in the ways of peace as they have proved courageous in the ways of war.

CITATION PRESENTED TO DR. JONAS SALK
April 22, 1955

For his remarkable contribution in developing the vaccine to
prevent paralytic poliomyelitis President Eisenhower presented
this citation to Dr. Jonas Salk, with the thanks of all Americans who
would be spared the fears of future epidemic.

[Citation read by the President]

Because of a signal and historic contribution to human welfare by Dr. Jonas E. Salk in his development of a vaccine to prevent paralytic poliomyelitis, I, Dwight D. Eisenhower, President of the United States, on behalf of the people of the United States, present to him this citation for his extraordinary achievement.

The work of Dr. Salk is in the highest tradition of selfless and dedicated medical research. He has provided a means for the control of a dread disease. By helping scientists in other countries with technical information; by offering to them the strains of seed virus and professional aid so that the production of vaccine can be started by them everywhere; by welcoming them to his laboratory that they may gain a fuller knowledge, Dr. Salk is a benefactor of mankind.

His achievement, a credit to our entire scientific community, does honor to all the people of the United States.

[Remarks of the President]

Dr. Salk, before I hand you this Citation, I should like to say to you that when I think of the countless thousands of American parents and grandparents who are hereafter to be spared the agonizing fears of the annual epidemic of poliomyelitis, when I think of all the agony that these people will be spared seeing their loved ones suffering in bed, I must say to you I have no words in which adequately to express the thanks of myself and all the people I know—all 164 million Americans, to say nothing of all the people in the world that will profit from your discovery. I am very, very happy to hand this to you.

STATEMENT ON DISARMAMENT
GENEVA CONFERENCE
July 21, 1955

President Eisenhower indicated that the United States had rapidly disarmed after World War II but had been forced to revamp her armed forces because of the world situation. The United States is willing to enter into an agreement for the reduction of armament. In particular the President addressed the Soviet Union, proposing several unique steps: exchange of complete blueprints of their respective military establishments and provision of facilities for aerial photography. The United States is prepared to begin a study and testing of a reliable inspection and reporting system.

Mr. Chairman (Nikolai Bulganin), Gentlemen:

Disarmament is one of the most important subjects on our agenda. It is also extremely difficult. In recent years the scientists have discovered methods of making weapons many, many times more destructive of opposing armed forces—but also of homes, and industries and lives—than ever known or even imagined before. These same scientific discoveries have made much more complex the problems of limitation and control and reduction of armament.

After our victory as Allies in World War II, my country rapidly disarmed. Within a few years our armament was at a very low level. Then events occurred beyond our borders which caused us to realize that we had disarmed too much. For our own security and to safeguard peace we needed greater strength. Therefore we proceeded to rearm and to associate with others in a partnership for peace and for mutual security.

The American people are determined to maintain and if necessary increase this armed strength for as long a period as is necessary to safeguard peace and to maintain our security.

But we know that a mutually dependable system for less armament on the part of all nations would be a better way to safeguard peace and to maintain our security.

It would ease the fears of war in the anxious hearts of people everywhere. It would lighten the burdens upon the backs of the people. It would make it possible for every nation, great and small, developed and less developed, to advance the standards of living of its people, to attain better food, and clothing, and shelter, more of education and larger enjoyment of life.

Therefore the United States government is prepared to enter into a sound and reliable agreement making possible the reduction of armament. I have directed that an intensive and thorough study of this subject be made within our own government. From these studies, which are continuing, a very important principle is emerging to which I referred in my opening statement on Monday.

No sound and reliable agreement can be made unless it is completely covered by an inspection and reporting system adequate to support every portion of the agreement.

The lessons of history teach us that disarmament agreements without adequate reciprocal inspection increase the dangers of war and do not brighten the prospects of peace.

Thus it is my view that the priority attention of our combined study of disarmament should be upon the subject of inspection and reporting.

Questions suggest themselves.

How effective an inspection system can be designed which would be mutually and reciprocally acceptable within our countries and the other nations of the world? How would such a system operate? What could it accomplish?

Is certainty against surprise aggression attainable by inspection? Could violations be discovered promptly and effectively counteracted?

We have not as yet been able to discover any scientific or other inspection method which would make certain of the elimination of nuclear weapons. So far as we are aware no other nation has made such a discovery. Our study of this problem is continuing. We have not as yet been able to discover any accounting or other inspection method of being certain of the true budgetary facts of total expenditures for armament. Our study of this problem is continuing. We by no means exclude the possibility of finding useful checks in these fields.

As you can see from these statements, it is our impression that many past proposals of disarmament are more sweeping than can be insured by effective inspection.

Gentlemen, since I have been working on this memorandum to present to this Conference, I have been searching my heart and mind for something that I could say here that could convince everyone of the great sincerity of the United States in approaching this problem of disarmament.

I should address myself for a moment principally to the Delegates from the Soviet Union, because our two great countries admittedly possess new and terrible weapons in quantities which do give rise in other parts of the world, or reciprocally, to the fears and dangers of surprise attack.

I propose, therefore, that we take a practical step, that we begin an arrangement, very quickly, as between ourselves—immediately. These steps would include:

To give to each other a complete blueprint of our military establishments, from beginning to end, from one end of our countries to the other; lay out the establishments and provide the blueprints to each other.

Next, to provide within our countries facilities for aerial photography to the other country—we to provide you the facilities within our country, ample facilities for aerial reconnaissance, where you can make all the pictures you choose and take them to your own country to study, you to provide exactly the same facilities for us and we to make these examinations, and by this step to convince the world that we are providing as between ourselves against the possibility of great surprise attack, thus lessening danger and relaxing tension. Likewise we will make more easily attainable a comprehensive and effective system of inspection and disarmament, because what I propose, I assure you, would be but a beginning.

Now from my statements I believe you will anticipate my suggestion. It is that we instruct our representatives in the Subcommittee on Disarmament in discharge of their mandate from the United Nations to give priority effort to the study of inspection and reporting. Such a study could well include a step by step testing of inspection and reporting methods.

The United States is ready to proceed in the study and testing of a reliable system of inspections and reporting, and when that system is proved, then to reduce armaments with all others to the extent that the system will provide assured results.

The successful working out of such a system would do much to develop the mutual confidence which will open wide the avenues of progress for all our peoples.

The quest for peace is the statesman's most exacting duty. Security of the nation entrusted to his care is his greatest responsibility. Practical progress to lasting peace is his fondest hope. Yet in pursuit of his hope he must not betray the trust placed in him as guardian of the people's security. A sound peace— with security, justice, wellbeing, and freedom for the people of the world—*can* be achieved, but only by patiently and thoughtfully following a hard and sure and tested road.

SPECIAL MESSAGE TO THE CONGRESS
THE SITUATION IN THE MIDDLE EAST
January 5, 1957

President Eisenhower indicated that the Russian interests in the Middle East were solely those of power politics. He asked Congress to join with him in warning the Communists that the United States would not tolerate any aggressive acts in the Middle East and would come to the aid of any nation threatened.

To the Congress of the United States:

. . . There is a special situation in the Middle East which I feel I should lay before you.

Before doing so it is well to remind ourselves that our basic national objective in international affairs remains peace—a world peace based on justice. . . .

The Middle East has abruptly reached a new and critical stage in its long and important history. In past decades many of the countries in that area were not fully self-governing. But since the First World War there has been a steady evolution toward self-government and independence. This development the United States has welcomed and has encouraged.

The evolution to independence has in the main been a peaceful process. But the area has been often troubled. Persistent cross-currents of distrust and fear with raids back and forth across national boundaries have brought about a high degree of instability in much of the Mid East. Just recently there have hostilities involving Western European nations that once exercised much influence in the area. Also the relatively large attack by Israel in October has intensified the basic differences between that nation and its Arab neighbors. All this instability has been heightened and, at times, manipulated by International Communism.

Russia's rulers have long sought to dominate the Middle East. The reasons are not hard to find. They do not affect Russia's security, for no one plans to use the Middle East as a base for aggression against Russia. Never for a moment has the United States entertained such a thought. . . .

That statement I make solemnly and emphatically.

Neither does Russia's desire to dominate the Middle East spring from its own economic interest in the area. Russia does not appreciably use or depend upon the Suez Canal. . . . The Soviets have no need for, and could provide no market for, the petroleum resources which constitute the principal natural wealth of the area. Indeed, the Soviet Union is a substantial exporter of petroleum products.

The reason for Russia's interest in the Middle East is solely that of power politics. . . .

This region has always been the crossroads of the continents of the Eastern Hemisphere. The Suez Canal enables the nations of Asia and Europe to carry on the commerce that is essential if these countries are to maintain well-rounded and prosperous economies. The Middle East provides a gateway between Eurasia and Africa.

It contains about two thirds of the presently known oil deposits of the world and it normally supplies the petroleum needs of many nations of Europe, Asia and Africa. The nations of Europe are peculiarly dependent upon this supply, and this dependency relates to transportation as well as to production! This has been vividly demonstrated since the closing of the Suez Canal and some of the pipelines. . . .

These things stress the immense importance of the Middle East. If the nations of that area should lose their independence, if they were dominated by alien forces hostile to freedom, that would be both a tragedy for the area and for many other free nations whose economic life would be subject to near strangulation. Western Europe would be endangered just as though there had been no Marshall Plan, no North Atlantic Treaty Organization. The free nations of Asia and Africa, too, would be placed in serious jeopardy. And the countries of the Middle East would lose the markets upon which their economies depend. All this would have the most adverse, if not disastrous, effect upon our own nation's economic life and political prospects.

Then there are other factors which transcend the material. The Middle East is the birthplace of three great religions—Moslem, Christian and Hebrew. Mecca and Jerusalem are more than places on the map. They symbolize religions which teach that the spirit has supremacy over matter and that the individual has a dignity and rights of which no despotic government can rightfully deprive him. It would be intolerable if the holy places of the Middle East should be subjected to a rule that glorifies atheistic materialism.

International Communism, of course, seeks to mask its purposes of domination by expressions of good will and by superficially attractive offers of political, economic and military aid. But any free nation, which is the subject of Soviet enticement, ought, in elementary wisdom, to look behind the mask. . . .

Thus, we have these simple and indisputable facts:

1. The Middle East, which has always been coveted by Russia, would today be prized more than ever by International Communism.

2. The Soviet rulers continue to show that they do not scruple to use any means to gain their ends.

3. The free nations of the Mid East need, and for the most part want, added strength to assure their continued independence.

Our thoughts naturally turn to the United Nations as a protector of small nations. Its charter gives it primary responsibility for the maintenance of international peace and security. Our country has given the United Nations its full support in relation to the hostilities in Hungary and in Egypt. The United Nations was able to bring about a cease-fire and withdrawal of hostile forces from Egypt because it was dealing with governments and peoples who had a decent respect for the opinions of mankind as reflected in the United Nations General Assembly. . . .The United Nations can always be helpful, but it cannot be a wholly dependable protector of freedom when the ambitions of the Soviet Union are involved.

Under all the circumstances I have laid before you, a greater responsibility now devolves upon the United States. We have shown, so that none can doubt, our dedication to the principle that force shall not be used internationally for any aggressive purpose and that the integrity and independence of the nations of the Middle East should be inviolate.

There is general recognition in the Middle East, as elsewhere, that the United States does not seek either political or economic domination over any other people. Our desire is a world environment of freedom, not servitude. On the other hand many, if not all, of the nations of the Middle East are aware of the danger that stems from International Communism and welcome closer cooperation with the United States to realize for themselves the United Nations goals of independence, economic well-being and spiritual growth.

If the Middle East is to continue its geographic role of uniting rather than separating East and West; if its vast economic resources are to serve the well-being of the peoples there, as well as that of others; and if its cultures and religions and their shrines are to be preserved for the uplifting of the spirits of the peoples, then the United States must make more evident its willingness to support the independence of the freedom-loving nations of the area.

Under these circumstances I deem it necessary to seek the cooperation of the Congress. Only with that cooperation can we give the reassurance needed to deter aggression, to give courage and confidence to those who are dedicated to freedom and thus prevent a chain of events which would gravely endanger all of the free world. . . .

Nevertheless, weaknesses in the present situation and the increased danger from International Communism, convince me that basic United States policy should now find expression in joint action by the Congress and the Executive. Furthermore, our joint resolve should be so couched as to make it apparent that if need be our words will be backed by action.

It is nothing new for the President and the Congress to join to recognize that the national integrity of other free nations is directly related to our own security. . . .

It is now essential that the United States should manifest through joint action of the President and the Congress our determination to assist those nations of the Mid East area, which desire that assistance.

The action which I propose would have the following features.

It would, first of all, authorize the United States to cooperate with and assist any nation or group of nations in the general area of the Middle East in the development of economic strength dedicated to the maintenance of national independence.

It would, in the second place, authorize the Executive to undertake in the same region programs of military assistance and cooperation with any nation or group of nations which desires such aid.

It would, in the third place, authorize such assistance and cooperation to include the employment of the armed forces of the United States to secure and protect the territorial integrity and political independence of such nations, requesting such aid, against overt armed aggression from any nation controlled by International Communism.

These measures would have to be consonant with the treaty obligations of the United States, including the Charter of the United Nations and with any action or recommendations of the United Nations. They would also, if armed attack occurs, be subject to the overriding authority of the United Nations Security Council in accordance with the Charter.

The present proposal would, in the fourth place, authorize the President to employ, for economic and defensive military purposes, sums available under the Mutual Security Act of 1954, as amended, without regard to existing limitations. . . .

This program will not solve all the problems of the Middle East. Neither does it represent the totality of our policies for the area. There are the problems of Palestine and relations between Israel and the Arab States, and the future of the Arab refugees. There is the problem of the future status of the Suez Canal. These difficulties are aggravated by International Communism, but they would exist quite apart from that threat. It is not the purpose of the legislation I propose to deal directly with these problems. The United Nations is actively concerning itself with all these matters, and we are supporting the United Nations. The United States has made clear, notably by Secretary Dulles' address of August 26, 1955, that we are willing to do much to assist the United Nations in solving the basic problems of Palestine.

The proposed legislation is primarily designed to deal with the possibility of Communist aggression, direct and indirect. There is imperative need that any lack of power in the area should be made good, not by external or alien force, but by the increased vigor and security of the independent nations of the area.

Experience shows that indirect aggression rarely if ever succeeds where there is reasonable security against direct aggression; where the government disposes of loyal security forces, and where economic conditions are such as not to make Communism seem an attractive alternative. The program I suggest deals with all three aspects of this matter and thus with the problem of indirect aggression.

It is my hope and belief that if our purpose be proclaimed, as proposed by the requested legislation, that very fact will serve to halt any contemplated aggression. . . .

And as I have indicated, it will also be necessary for us to contribute economically to strengthen those countries, or groups of countries, which have governments manifestly dedicated to the preservation of independence and resistance to subversion. Such measures will provide the greatest insurance against Communist inroads. Words alone are not enough. . . .

In the situation now existing, the greatest risk, as is often the case, is that ambitious despots may miscalculate. If power-hungry Communists should either falsely or correctly estimate that the Middle East is inadequately defended, they might be tempted to use open measures of armed attack. If so, that would start a chain of circumstances which would almost surely involve the United States in military action. I am convinced that the best insurance against this dangerous contingency is to make clear now our readiness to cooperate fully and freely with our friends of the Middle East in ways consonant with the purposes and principles of the United Nations. I intend promptly to send a special mission to the Middle East to explain the cooperation we are prepared to give. . . .

FIFTH ANNUAL MESSAGE
January 10, 1957

The President reviewed the economic, political, and diplomatic developments during his first term in office. He reiterated his request of the previous year that the Congress enact a strong civil rights program. He also requested that Congress cooperate in helping the United States to maintain its leading role in international affairs.

To the Congress of the United States:

I appear before the Congress today to report on the state of the Union and the relationships of the Union to the other nations of the world. . . .

The forces now at work in the minds and hearts of men will not be spent through many years. In the main, today's expressions of nationalism are, in spirit, echoes of our forefathers' struggle for independence.

This Republic cannot be aloof to these events heralding a new epoch in the affairs of mankind. . . .

The state of the Union, at the opening of the 85th Congress, continues to vindicate the wisdom of the principles on which this Republic is founded. Proclaimed in the Constitution of the Nation and in many of our historic documents, and founded in devout religious convictions, these principles enunciate:

A vigilant regard for human liberty.

A wise concern for human welfare.

A ceaseless effort for human progress.

Fidelity to these principles, in our relations with other peoples, has won us new friendships and has increased our opportunity for service within the family of nations. The appeal of these principles is universal, lighting fires in the souls of men everywhere. We shall continue to uphold them against those who deny them and in counseling with our friends. . . .

Through the past 4 years these principles have guided the legislative programs submitted by the Administration to the Congress. As we attempt to apply them to current events, domestic and foreign, we must take into account the complex entity that is the United States of America; what endangers it: what can improve it. . . .

Our economy is strong, expanding, and fundamentally sound. But in any realistic appraisal, even the optimistic analyst will realize that in a prosperous period the principal threat to efficient functioning of a free enterprise system is inflation. We look back on 4 years of prosperous activities during which prices, the cost of living, have been relatively stable—that is, inflation has been held in check. But it is clear that the danger is always present, particularly if the Government might become profligate in its expenditures or private groups might ignore all the possible results on our economy of unwise struggles for immediate gain.

This danger requires a firm resolution that the Federal Government shall utilize only a prudent share of the Nation's resources, that it shall live within its means, carefully measuring against need alternative proposals for expenditures.

Through the next 4 years, I shall continue to insist that the executive departments and agencies of Government search out additional ways to save money and manpower. I urge that the Congress be equally watchful in this matter.

We pledge the Government's share in guarding the integrity of the dollar. But the Government's efforts cannot be the entire campaign against inflation, the thief that can rob the individual of the value of the pension and social security he has earned during his productive life. For success, Government's efforts must be paralleled by the attitudes and actions of individual citizens. . . .

I call on leaders in business and in labor to think well on their responsibility to the American people. With all elements of our society, they owe the Nation a vigilant guard against the inflationary tendencies that are always at work in a dynamic economy operating at today's high levels. They can powerfully help counteract or accentuate such tendencies by their wage and price policies.

Business in its pricing policies should avoid unnecessary price increases, especially at a time like the present when demand in so many areas presses hard on short supplies. A reasonable profit is essential to the new investments that provide more jobs in an expanding economy. But business leaders must, in the national interest, studiously avoid those price rises that are possible only because of vital or unusual needs of the whole Nation.

If our economy is to remain healthy, increases in wages and other labor benefits, negotiated by labor and management, must be reasonably related to improvements in productivity. Such increases are beneficial, for they provide wage earners with greater purchasing power. Except where necessary to correct obvious injustices, wage increases that outrun productivity, however, are an inflationary factor. Wage negotiations should also take cognizance of the right of the public generally to share in the benefits of improvements in technology.

Freedom has been defined as the opportunity for self-discipline. This definition has a special application to the areas of wage and price policy in a free economy. Should we persistently fail to discipline ourselves, eventually there will be increasing pressure on Government to redress the failure. By that process freedom will step by step disappear. No subject on the domestic scene should more attract the concern of the friends of American working men and women and of free business enterprise than the forces that threaten a steady depreciation of the value of our money. . . .

In all domestic matters, I believe that the people of the United States will expect of us effective action to remedy past failure in meeting critical needs.

High priority should be given the school construction bill. This will benefit children of all races throughout the country—and children of all races need schools now. A program designed to meet emergency needs for more classrooms should be enacted without delay. . . .

I should say here that we have much reason to be proud of the progress our people are making in mutual understanding—the chief buttress of human and civil rights. Steadily we are moving closer to the goal of fair and equal treatment of citizens without regard to race or color. But unhappily much remains to be done.

Last year the administration recommended to the Congress a four-point program to reinforce civil rights. That program included—

(1) Creation of a bipartisan commission to investigate asserted violations of civil rights and to make recommendations;

(2) Creation of a civil rights division in the Department of Justice in charge of an Assistant Attorney General;

(3) Enactment by the Congress of new laws to aid in the enforcement of voting rights; and

(4) Amendment of the laws so as to permit the Federal Government to seek from the civil courts preventive relief in civil rights cases.

I urge that the Congress enact this legislation.

Essential to the stable economic growth we seek is a system of well-adapted and efficient financial institutions. I believe the time has come to conduct a broad national inquiry into the nature, performance, and adequacy of our financial system, both in terms of its direct service to the whole economy and in terms of its function as the mechanism through which monetary and credit policy takes effect. I believe the Congress should authorize the creation of a commission of able and qualified citizens to undertake this vital inquiry. Out of their findings and recommendations the administration would develop and present to the Congress any legislative proposals that might be indicated for the purpose of improving our financial machinery. . . .

Turning to the international scene:

The existence of a strongly armed imperialistic dictatorship poses a continuing threat to the free world's and thus to our own Nation's security and peace. There are certain truths to be remembered here.

First, America alone and isolated cannot assure even its own security. We must be joined by the capability and resolution of nations that have proved themselves dependable defenders of freedom. Isolation from them invites war. Our security is also enhanced by the immeasurable interest that joins us with all peoples who believe that peace with justice must be preserved, that wars of agression are crimes against humanity.

Another truth is that our survival in today's world requires modern, adequate, dependable military strength. Our Nation has made great strides in assuring a modern defense, so armed in new weapons, so deployed, so equipped, that today our security force is the most powerful in our peacetime history. It can punish heavily any enemy who undertakes to attack us. It is a major deterrent to war.

By our research and development more efficient weapons—some of amazing capabilities—are being constantly created. These vital efforts we shall continue. Yet we must not delude ourselves that safety necessarily increases as expenditures for military research or forces in being go up. Indeed, beyond a wise and reasonable level, which is always changing and is under constant study, money spent on arms may be money wasted on sterile metal or inflated costs, thereby weakening the very security and strength we seek. . . .

The finest military establishment we can produce must work closely in cooperation with the forces of our friends. Our system of regional pacts, developed within the Charter of the United Nations, serves to increase both our own security and the security of other nations. . . .

With other free nations, we should vigorously prosecute measures that will promote mutual strength, prosperity, and welfare within the free world. Strength is essentially a product of economic health and social well-being. Consequently, even as we continue our programs of military assistance, we must emphasize aid to our friends in building more productive economies and in better satisfying the natural demands of their people for progress. Thereby we shall move a long way toward a peaceful world.

A sound and safeguarded agreement for open skies, unarmed aerial sentinels, and reduced armament would provide a valuable contribution toward a durable peace in the years ahead. We are willing to enter any reliable agreement which would reverse the trend toward ever more devastating nuclear weapons; reciprocally provide against the possibility of surpise attack; mutually control the outer-space missile and satellite development; and make feasible a lower level of armaments and armed forces and an easier burden of military expenditures. Our continuing negotiations in this field are a major part of our quest for a confident peace in this atomic age. . . .

An essential step in this field is the provision of an administrative agency to insure the orderly and proper operation of existing arrangements under which multilateral trade is now carried on. To that end I urge congressional authorization for United States membership in the proposed Organization for Trade Cooperation, an action which will speed removal of discrimination against our export trade.

We welcome the efforts of a number of our European friends to achieve an integrated community to develop a common market. We likewise welcome their cooperative effort in the field of atomic energy.

To demonstrate once again our unalterable purpose to make of the atom a peaceful servant of humanity, I shortly shall ask the Congress to authorize full United States participation in the International Atomic Energy Agency.

World events have magnified both the responsibilities and the opportunities of the United States Information Agency. Just as, in recent months, the voice of communism has become more shaken and confused, the voice of truth must be more clearly heard. To enable our Information Agency to cope with these new responsibilities and opportunities, I am asking the Congress to increase appreciably the appropriations for this program and for legislation establishing a career service for the Agency's overseas Foreign Service officers.

The recent historic events in Hungary demand that all free nations share to the extent of their capabilities in the responsibility of granting asylum to victims of Communist persecution. I request the Congress promptly to enact legislation to regularize the status in the United States of Hungarian refugees brought here as parolees. I shall shortly recommend to the Congress by special message the changes in our immigration laws that I deem necessary in the light of our world responsibilities.

The cost of peace is something we must face boldly, fearlessly. Beyond money, it involves changes in attitudes, the renunciation of old prejudices, even the sacrifice of some seeming self-interest.

Only 5 days ago I expressed to you the grave concern of your Government over the threat of Soviet aggression in the Middle East. I asked for congressional authorization to help counter this threat. I say again that this matter is of vital and immediate importance to the Nation's and the free world's security and peace. By our proposed programs in the Middle East, we hope to assist in establishing a climate in which constructive and long-term solutions to basic problems of the area may be sought. . . .

No reasonable man will question the absolute need for our American neighbors to be prosperous and secure. Their security and prosperity are inextricably bound to our own. And we are, of course, already joined with these neighbors by historic pledges.

Again, no reasonable man will deny that the freedom and prosperity and security of Western Europe are vital to our own prosperity and security. If the institutions, the skills, the manpower of its peoples were to fall under the domination of an aggressive imperialism, the violent change in the balance of world power and in the pattern of world commerce could not be fully compensated for by any American measures, military or economic.

But these people, whose economic strength is largely dependent on free and uninterrupted movement of oil from the Middle East, cannot prosper— indeed, their economies would be severely impaired—should that area be controlled by an enemy and the movement of oil be subject to its decisions.

Next, to the eastward, are Asiatic and far eastern peoples, recently returned to independent control of their own affairs or now emerging into sovereign statehood. Their potential strength constitutes new assurance for stability and peace in the world—if they can retain their independence. Should they lose freedom and be dominated by an aggressor, the worldwide effects would imperil the security of the free world.

In short, the world has so shrunk that all free nations are our neighbors. Without cooperative neighbors, the United States cannot maintain its own security and welfare, because—

First, America's vital interests are worldwide, embracing both hemispheres and every continent.

Second, we have community of interest with every nation in the free world.

Third, interdependence of interests requires a decent respect for the rights and the peace of all peoples.

These principles motivate our actions within the United Nations. There, before all the world, by our loyalty to them, by our practice of them, let us strive to set a standard to which all who seek justice and who hunger for peace can rally. . . .

SECOND INAUGURAL ADDRESS
January 21, 1957

In this address President Eisenhower dedicated himself and the nation to a campaign to achieve peace and justice throughout the world. The American people must be willing to make sacrifices to gain peace and tranquillity.

Mr. Chairman, Mr. Vice President, Mr. Chief Justice, Mr. Speaker, members of my family and friends, my countrymen, and the friends of my country wherever they may be:

We meet again, as upon a like moment four years ago, and again you have witnessed my solemn oath of service to you.

I, too, am a witness, today testifying in your name to the principles and purposes to which we, as a people, are pledged.

Before all else, we seek, upon our common labor as a nation, the blessings of Almighty God. And the hopes in our hearts fashion the deepest prayers of our whole people.

May we pursue the right—without self-righteousness.

May we know unity—without conformity.

May we grow in strength—without pride in self.

May we, in our dealings with all peoples of the earth, ever speak truth and serve justice.

And so shall America—in the sight of all men of good will—prove true to the honorable purposes that bind and rule us as a people in all this time of trial through which we pass.

We live in a land of plenty, but rarely has this earth known such peril as today.

In our nation work and wealth abound. Our population grows. Commerce crowds our rivers and rails, our skies, harbors and highways. Our soil is fertile, our agriculture productive. The air rings with the song of our industry—rolling mills and blast furnaces, dynamos, dams and assembly lines—the chorus of America the bountiful.

Now this is our home—yet this is not the whole of our world. For our world is where our full destiny lies—with men, of all peoples and all nations, who are or would be free. And for them—and so for us—this is no time of ease or of rest.

In too much of the earth there is want, discord, danger. New forces and new nations stir and strive across the earth, with power to bring, by their fate, great good or great evil to the free world's future. From the deserts of North Africa to the islands of the South Pacific one third of all mankind has entered upon an historic struggle for a new freedom: freedom from grinding poverty. Across all continents, nearly a billion people seek, sometimes almost in desperation, for the skills and knowledge and assistance by which they may satisfy from their own resources, the material wants common to all mankind.

No nation, however old or great, escapes this tempest of change and turmoil. Some, impoverished by the recent World War, seek to restore their means of livelihood. In the heart of Europe, Germany still stands tragically divided. So is the whole continent divided. And so, too, all the world.

The divisive force is International Communism and the power that it controls.

The designs of that power, dark in purpose, are clear in practice. It strives to seal forever the fate of those it has enslaved. It strives to break the ties that unite the free. And it strives to capture—to exploit for its own greater power —all forces of change in the world, especially the needs of the hungry and the hopes of the oppressed.

Yet the world of International Communism has itself been shaken by a fierce and mighty force: the readiness of men who love freedom to pledge their lives to that love. Through the night of their bondage, the unconquerable will of heroes has struck with the swift, sharp thrust of lightning. Budapest is no longer merely the name of a city; henceforth it is a new and shining symbol of man's yearing to be free.

Thus across all the globe there harshly blow the winds of change. And, we —though fortunate be our lot—know that we can never turn our backs to them.

We look upon this shaken earth, and we declare our firm and fixed purpose—the building of a peace with justice in a world where moral law prevails.

The building of such a peace is a bold and solemn purpose. To proclaim it is easy. To serve it will be hard. And to attain it, we must be aware of its full meaning—and ready to pay its full price.

We know clearly what we seek, and why.

We seek peace, knowing that peace is the climate of freedom. And now, as in no other age, we seek it because we have been warned, by the power of modern weapons, that peace may be the only climate possible for human life itself.

Yet this peace we seek cannot be born of fear alone: it must be rooted in the lives of nations. There must be justice, sensed and shared by all people, for, without justice the world can know only a tense and unstable truce. There must be law, steadily invoked and respected by all nations, for without law, the world promises only such meager justice as the pity of the strong upon the weak. But the law of which we speak, comprehending the values of freedom, affirms the equality of all nations, great and small.

Splendid as can be the blessings of such a peace, high will be its cost: in toil patiently sustained, in help honorably given, in sacrifice calmly borne.

We are called to meet the price of this peace.

To counter the threat of those who seek to rule by force, we must pay the costs of our own needed military strength, and help to build the security of others.

We must use our skills and knowledge and, at times, our substance, to help others rise from misery, however far the scene of suffering may be from our shores. For wherever in the world a people knows desperate want, there must appear at least the spark of hope, the hope of progress—or there will surely rise at last the flames of conflict.

We recognize and accept our own deep involvement in the destiny of men everywhere. We are accordingly pledged to honor, and to strive to fortify, the authority of the United Nations. For in that body rests the best hope of our age for the assertion of that law by which all nations may live in dignity.

And beyond this general resolve, we are called to act a responsible role in the world's great concerns or conflicts—whether they touch upon the affairs of a vast region, the fate of an island in the Pacific, or the use of a canal in the Middle East. Only in respecting the hopes and cultures of others will we practice the equality of all nations. Only as we show willingness and wisdom in giving counsel—in receiving counsel—and in sharing burdens, will we wisely perform the work of peace.

For one truth must rule all we think and all we do. No people can live to itself alone. The unity of all who dwell in freedom is their only sure defense. The economic need of all nations—in mutual dependence—makes isolation an impossibility: not even America's prosperity could long survive if other nations did not also prosper. No nation can longer be a fortress, lone and strong and safe. And any people, seeking such shelter for themselves, can now build only their own prison.

Our pledge to these principles is constant, because we believe in their rightness.

We do not fear this world of change. America is no stranger to much of its spirit. Everywhere we see the seeds of the same growth that America itself has known. The American experiment has, for generations, fired the passion and the courage of millions elsewhere seeking freedom, equality, opportunity. And the American story of material progress has helped excite the longing of all needy peoples for some satisfaction of their human wants. These hopes that we have helped to inspire, we can help to fulfill.

In this confidence, we speak plainly to all peoples.

We cherish our friendship with all nations that are or would be free. We respect, no less, their independence. And when, in time of want or peril, they ask our help, they may honorably receive it; for we no more seek to buy their sovereignty than we would sell our own. Sovereignty is never bartered among free men.

We honor the aspirations of those nations which, now captive, long for freedom. We seek neither their military alliance nor any artificial imitation of our society. And they can know the warmth of the welcome that awaits them when, as must be, they join again the ranks of freedom.

We honor, no less in this divided world than in a less tormented time, the people of Russia. We do not dread, rather do we welcome, their progress in education and industry. We wish them success in their demands for more intellectual freedom, greater security before their own laws, fuller enjoyment of the rewards of their own toil. For as such things come to pass, the more certain will be the coming of that day when our peoples may freely meet in friendship.

So we voice our hope and our belief that we can help to heal this divided world. Thus may the nations cease to live in trembling before the menace of force. Thus may the weight of fear and the weight of arms be taken from the burdened shoulders of mankind.

This, nothing less, is the labor to which we are called and our strength dedicated.

And so the prayer of our people carries far beyond our own frontiers, to the wide world of our duty and our destiny.

May the light of freedom, coming to all darkened lands, flame brightly— until at last the darkness is no more.

May the turbulence of our age yield to a true time of peace, when men and nations shall share a life that honors the dignity of each, the brotherhood of all.

Thank you very much.

RADIO AND TELEVISION ADDRESS
TO THE AMERICAN PEOPLE
THE SITUATION IN LITTLE ROCK
September 24, 1957

Indicating that disorderly mobs prevented the carrying out of Federal Court orders in regard to public school desegregation, President Eisenhower stated that he had issued a proclamation calling upon the mob to disperse. He then went on to discuss the problems concerned with desegregation of schools in Little Rock, Arkansas, since May, 1955. Violence flies in the face of American tradition and damages the public image at a time when serious crises are being faced abroad.

Good Evening, My Fellow Citizens:

For a few minutes this evening I want to speak to you about the serious situation that has arisen in Little Rock. To make this talk I have come to the President's office in the White House. I could have spoken from Rhode Island, where I have been staying recently, but I felt that, in speaking from the house of Lincoln, of Jackson and of Wilson, my words would better convey both the sadness I feel in the action I was compelled today to take and the firmness with which I intend to pursue this course until the orders of the Federal Court at Little Rock can be executed without unlawful interference.

In that city, under the leadership of demagogic extremists, disorderly mobs have deliberately prevented the carrying out of proper orders from a Federal Court. Local authorities have not eliminated that violent opposition and, under the law, I yesterday issued a proclamation calling upon the mob to disperse.

This morning the mob again gathered in front of the Central High School of Little Rock, obviously for the purpose of again preventing the carrying out of the Court's order relating to the admission of Negro children to that school.

Whenever normal agencies prove inadequate to the task and it becomes necessary for the Executive Branch of the Federal Government to use its powers and authority to uphold Federal Courts, the President's responsibility is inescapable.

In accordance with that responsibility, I have today issued an Executive Order directing the use of troops under Federal authority to aid in the execution of Federal law at Little Rock, Arkansas. This became necessary when my proclamation of yesterday was not observed, and the obstruction of justice still continues.

It is important that the reasons for my action be understood by all our citizens.

As you know, the Supreme Court of the United States has decided that separate public educational facilities for the races are inherently unequal and therefore compulsory school segregation laws are unconstitutional.

Our personal opinions about the decision have no bearing on the matter of enforcement; the responsibility and authority of the Supreme Court to interpret the Constitution are very clear. Local Federal Courts were instructed to issue such orders and decrees as might be necessary to achieve admission to public schools without regard to race—and with all deliberate speed.

During the past several years, many communities in our Southern States have instituted public school plans for gradual progress in the enrollment and attendance of school children of all races in order to bring themselves into compliance with the law of the land.

They thus demonstrated to the world that we are a nation in which laws, not men, are supreme.

I regret to say that this truth—the cornerstone of our liberties—was not observed in this instance.

It was my hope that this localized situation would be brought under control by city and state authorities. If the use of local police powers had been sufficient, our traditional method of leaving the problems in those hands would have been pursued. But when large gatherings of obstructionists made it impossible for the decrees of the Court to be carried out, both the law and the national interest demanded that the President take action.

Here is the sequence of events in the development of the Little Rock school case.

In May of 1955, the Little Rock School Board approved a moderate plan for the gradual desegregation of the public schools in that city. It provided that a start toward integration would be made at the present term in the high school, and that the plan would be in full operation by 1963. Here I might say that in a number of communities in Arkansas integration in the schools has already started and without violence of any kind. Now this Little Rock plan was challenged in the courts by some who believed that the period of time as proposed in the plan was too long.

The United States Court at Little Rock, which has supervisory responsibility under the law for the plan of desegregation in the public schools, dismissed the challenge, thus approving a gradual rather than an abrupt change from the existing system. The court found that the school board had acted in good faith in planning for a public school system free from racial discrimination.

Since that time, the court has on three separate occasions issued orders directing that the plan be carried out. All persons were instructed to refrain from interfering with the efforts of the school board to comply with the law.

Proper and sensible observance of the law then demanded the respectful obedience which the nation has a right to expect from all its people. This, unfortunately, has not been the case at Little Rock. Certain misguided persons, many of them imported into Little Rock by agitators, have insisted upon defying the law and have sought to bring it into disrepute. The orders of the court have thus been frustrated.

The very basis of our individual rights and freedoms rests upon the certainty that the President and the Executive Branch of Government will support and insure the carrying out of the decisions of the Federal Courts, even, when necessary with all the means at the President's command.

Unless the President did so, anarchy would result.

There would be no security for any except that which each one of us could provide for himself.

The interest of the nation in the proper fulfillment of the law's requirements cannot yield to opposition and demonstrations by some few persons.

Mob rule cannot be allowed to override the decisions of our courts.

Now, let me make it very clear that Federal troops are not being used to relieve local and state authorities of their primary duty to preserve the peace and order of the community. Nor are the troops there for the purpose of taking over the responsibility of the School Board and the other responsible local officials in running Central High School. The running of our school system and the maintenance of peace and order in each of our States are strictly local affairs and the Federal Government does not interfere except in a very few special cases and when requested by one of the several States. In the present case the troops are there, pursuant to law, solely for the purpose of preventing interference with the orders of the Court.

The proper use of the powers of the Executive Branch to enforce the orders of a Federal Court is limited to extraordinary and compelling circumstances. Manifestly, such an extreme situation has been created in Little Rock. This challenge must be met and with such measures as will preserve to the people as a whole their lawfully-protected rights in a climate permitting their free and fair exercise.

The overwhelming majority of our people in every section of the country are united in their respect for observance of the law—even in those cases where they may disagree with that law.

They deplore the call of extremists to violence.

The decision of the Supreme Court concerning school integration, of course, affects the South more seriously than it does other sections of the country. In that region I have many warm friends, some of them in the city of Little Rock. I have deemed it a great personal privilege to spend in our Southland tours of duty while in the military service and enjoyable recreational periods since that time.

So from intimate personal knowledge, I know that the overwhelming majority of the people in the South—including those of Arkansas and of Little Rock—are of good will, united in their efforts to preserve and respect the law even when they disagree with it.

They do not sympathise with mob rule. They, like the rest of our nation, have proved in two great wars their readiness to sacrifice for America.

A foundation of our American way of life is our national respect for law.

In the South, as elsewhere, citizens are keenly aware of the tremendous disservice that has been done to the people of Arkansas in the eyes of the nation, and that has been done to the nation in the eyes of the world.

At a time when we face grave situations abroad because of the hatred that Communism bears toward a system of government based on human rights, it would be difficult to exaggerate the harm that is being done to the prestige and influence, and indeed to the safety, of our nation and the world.

Our enemies are gloating over this incident and using it everywhere to misrepresent our whole nation. We are portrayed as a violator of those standards of conduct which the peoples of the world united to proclaim in the Charter of the United Nations. There they affirmed "faith in fundamental human rights" and "in the dignity and worth of the human person" and they did so "without distinction as to race, sex, language or religion."

And so, with deep confidence, I call upon the citizens of the State of Arkansas to assist in bringing to an immediate end all interference with the law and its processes. If resistance to the Federal Court orders ceases at once, the further presence of Federal troops will be unnecessary and the City of Little Rock will return to its normal habits of peace and order and a blot upon the fair name and high honor of our nation in the world will be removed.

Thus will be restored the image of America and of all its parts as one nation, indivisible, with liberty and justice for all.

Good night, and thank you very much.

LETTER TO NIKOLAI BULGANIN, CHAIRMAN
COUNCIL OF MINISTERS, U.S.S.R.
January 13, 1958

President Eisenhower first dismissed the issue of which of the two nations desires peace more. He maintained that the past forty years had shown the interest of the United States in peace—how it was unprepared or ill-prepared on all three occasions when war came. The President assured the Chairman that the United States would never support any aggression by any collective defense organization, and that the United States would move toward development of effective collective security measures through the United Nations. The Chairman seemed to ignore the obligations of the United Nations Charter in his proposals. The President in turn proposed that the United Nations be strengthened; that agreements regarding Germany and Eastern Europe be arranged; and that the Soviet Union and the United States agree that outer space should be used only for peaceful purposes. Finally the President indicated that he could not see that a summit conference would be valuable at this point.

Dear Mr. Chairman:

When on December tenth I received your communication, I promptly acknowledged it with the promise that I would in due course give you a considered reply. I now do so.

Your communication seems to fall into three parts: the need for peace; your contention that peace is endangered by the collective self-defense efforts of free world nations; and your specific proposals. I shall respond in that same order and make my own proposals.

Peace and good will among men have been the heartfelt desire of peoples since time immemorial. But professions of peace by governmental leaders have not always been a dependable guide to their actual intentions. Moreover, it seems to me to be profitless for us to debate the question of which of our two governments wants peace the more. Both of us have asserted that our respective peoples ardently desire peace and perhaps you and I feel this same urge equally. The heart of the matter becomes the determination of the terms on which the maintenance of peace can be assured, and the confidence that each of us can justifiably feel that these terms will be respected.

In the United States the people and their government desire peace and in this country the people exert such constitutional control over government that no government could possibly initiate aggressive war. Under authority already given by our Congress, the United States can and would respond at once if we or any of our allies were attacked. But the United States cannot initiate war without the prior approval of the peoples' representatives in the Congress. This process requires time and public debate. Not only would our people repudiate any effort to begin an attack, but the element of surprise, so important in any aggressive move, would be wholly lacking. Aggressive war by us is not only abhorrent; it is impractical and impossible.

The past forty years provide an opportunity to judge the comparative peace records of our two systems. We gladly submit our national record for respecting peace to the impartial judgment of mankind. I can assure you, Mr. Chairman, that in the United States the waging of peace has priority in every aspect, and every element, of our national life.

You argue that the danger of war is increased because the United States and other free world nations seek security on a collective basis and on the basis of military preparedness.

Three times in this century wars have occurred under circumstances which strongly suggest, if indeed they do not prove, that war would not have occurred had the United States been militarily strong and committed in advance to the defense of nations that were attacked.

On each of these three occasions when war came, the United States was militarily unprepared, or ill-prepared, and it was not known that the United States would go to the aid of those subjected to armed aggression. Yet now it appears, Mr. Chairman, that you contend that weakness and disunity would make war less likely.

I may be permitted perhaps to recall that in March 1939, when the Soviet Union felt relatively weak and threatened by Fascist aggression, it contended that aggression was rife because "the majority of the non-aggressive countries, particularly England and France, have rejected the policy of collective security," and Stalin went on to say that the policy of "Let each country defend itself as it likes and as best it can ... means conniving at aggression, giving free rein to war."

Now the Soviet Union is no longer weak or confronted by powerful aggressive forces. The vast Sino-Soviet bloc embraces nearly one billion people and large resources. Such a bloc would of course be dominant in the world were the free world nations to be disunited.

It is natural that any who want to impose their system on the world should prefer that those outside that system should be weak and divided. But that expansionist policy cannot be sanctified by protestations of peace.

Of course the United States would greatly prefer it if collective security could be obtained on a universal basis through the United Nations.

This was the hope when in 1945 our two governments and others signed the Charter of the United Nations, conferring upon its Security Council primary responsibility for the maintenance of international peace and security. Also, by that Charter we agreed to make available to the Security Council armed forces, assistance and facilities so that the Council could maintain and restore international peace and security.

The Soviet Union has persistently prevented the establishment of such a universal collective security system and has, by its use of the veto—now 82 times—made the Security Council undependable as a protector of the peace.

The possibility that the Security Council might become undependable was feared at the San Francisco Conference on World Organization, and accordingly the Charter recognized that, in addition to reliance on the Security Council, the nations possessed and might exercise an inherent right of collective self-defense. It has therefore been found not only desirable but necessary, if the free nations are to be secure and safe, to concert their defensive measures.

I can and do give you, Mr. Chairman, two solemn and categorical assurances.

(1) *Never* will the United States lend its support to any aggressive action by any collective defense organization or any member thereof;

(2) *Always* will the United States be ready to move toward the development of effective United Nations collective security measures in replacement of regional collective defense measures.

I turn now to consider your specific proposals.

I am compelled to conclude after the most careful study of your proposals that they seem to be unfortunately inexact or incomplete in their meaning and inadequate as a program for productive negotiations for peace.

You first seem to assume that the obligations of the Charter are non-existent and that the voice of the United Nations is nothing that we need to heed.

You suggest that we should agree to respect the independence of the countries of the Near and Middle East and renounce the use of force in the settlement of questions relating to the Near and Middle East. But by the Charter of the United Nations we have already taken precisely those obligations as regards all countries, including those of the Near and Middle East. Our profound hope is that the Soviets feel themselves as bound by the provisions of the Charter as, I assure you, we feel bound.

You also suggest submitting to the member states of NATO and the Warsaw Pact some form of non-aggression agreement. But all of the members of NATO are already bound to the United Nations Charter provision against aggression.

You suggest that the United States, the United Kingdom and the Soviet Union should undertake not to use *nuclear* weapons. But our three nations and others have already undertaken, by the Charter, not to use any weapons against the territorial integrity or political independence of *any* state. Our profound hope is that no weapons will be used by any country for such an indefensible purpose and that the Soviet Union will feel a similar aversion to any kind of aggression.

You suggest that we should proclaim our intention to develop between us relations of friendship and peaceful cooperation. Such an intention is indeed already proclaimed as between ourselves and others by the Charter of the United Nations to which we have subscribed. The need is, not to repeat what we already proclaim, but, Mr. Chairman, to take concrete steps under the present terms of the Charter, that will bring about these relations of friendship and peaceful cooperation. As recently as last November, the Communist Party of the Soviet Union signed and proclaimed to the world a declaration which was designed to promote the triumph of Communism throughout the world by every means not excluding violence, and which contained many slanderous references to the United States. I am bound to point out that such a declaration is difficult to reconcile with professions of a desire for friendship or indeed of peaceful coexistence. This declaration makes clear where responsibility for the "Cold War" lies.

You propose that we broaden the ties between us of a "scientific cultural and athletic" character. But already our two countries are negotiating for peaceful contacts even broader than "scientific, cultural and athletic." We hope for a positive result, even though in 1955, after the Summit Conference, when negotiations for such contacts were pressed by our Foreign Ministers at Geneva, the accomplishments were zero. It is above all important that our peoples should learn the true facts about each other. An informed public opinion in both our countries is essential to the proper understanding of our discussions.

You propose that we develop "normal" trade relations as part of the "peaceful cooperation" of which you speak. We welcome trade that carries no political or warlike implications. We do have restrictions on dealings in goods which are of war significance, but we impose no obstacles to peaceful trade.

Your remaining proposals relate to armament. In this connection, I note with deep satisfaction that you oppose "competition in the production of ever newer types of weapons." When I read that statement I expected to go on to read proposals to stop such production. But I was disappointed.

You renew the oft-repeated Soviet proposal that the United States, the United Kingdom and the Soviet Union should cease for two or three years to test nuclear weapons; and you suggest that nuclear weapons should not be stationed or produced in Germany. You add the possibility that Poland and Czechoslovakia might be added to this non-nuclear weapons area.

These proposals do not serve to meet the real problem of armament. The heart of that problem is, as you say, the mounting *production*, primarily by the Soviet Union and the United States, of new types of weapons.

Your proposal regarding Central Europe will of course be studied by

NATO and the NATO countries directly involved from the standpoint of its military and political implications. But there cannot be great significance in de-nuclearizing a small area when, as you say, "the range of modern types of weapons does not know of any geographical limit," and when you defer to the indefinite future any measures to stop the production of such weapons.

I note, furthermore, that your proposal on Germany is in no way related to the ending of the division of that country but would, in fact, tend to perpetuate that division. It is unrealistic thus to ignore the basic link between political solutions and security arrangements.

Surely, Mr. Chairman, at a time when we share great responsibility for shaping the development of the international situation, we can and must do better than what you propose.

In this spirit, I submit some proposals of my own.

(1) I propose that we strengthen the United Nations.

This organization and the pledges of its members embodied in the Charter constitute man's best hope for peace and justice. The United States feels bound by its solemn undertaking to act in accordance with the Principles of the Charter. Will not the Soviet Union clear away the doubt that it also feels bound by its Charter undertakings? And may we not perhaps go further and build up the authority of the United Nations?

Too often its recommendations go unheeded.

I propose, Mr. Chairman, that we should rededicate ourselves to the United Nations, its Principles and Purposes and to our Charter obligations. But I would do more.

Too often the Security Council is prevented, by veto, from discharging the primary responsibility we have given it for the maintenance of international peace and security. This prevention even extends to proposing procedures for the pacific settlement of disputes.

I propose that we should make it the policy of our two governments at least not to use veto power to prevent the Security Council from proposing methods for the pacific settlement of disputes pursuant to Chapter VI.

Nothing, I am convinced, would give the world more justifiable hope than the conviction that both of our governments are genuinely determined to make the United Nations the effective instrument of peace and justice that was the original design.

(2) If confidence is to be restored, there needs, above all, to be confidence in the pledged word. To us it appears that such confidence is lamentably lacking. That is conspicuously so in regard to two areas where the situation is a cause of grave international concern.

I refer first of all to Germany. This was the principal topic of our meeting of July 1955 and the only substantive agreement which was recorded in our agreed Directive was this:

"The Heads of Government, recognizing their common responsibility for the settlement of the German question and the reunification of Germany, have agreed that the settlement of the German question and the reunification of Germany by means of free elections shall be carried out in conformity with the national interests of the German people and the interests of European security."

In spite of our urging, your government has, for now two and one half years, taken no steps to carry out that agreement or to discharge that recognized responsibility. Germany remains forcibly divided.

This constitutes a great error, incompatible with European security. It also undermines confidence in the sanctity of our international agreements.

I therefore urge that we now proceed vigorously to bring about the reunification of Germany by free elections, as we agreed, and as the situation urgently demands.

I assure you that this act of simple justice and of good faith need not lead to any increased jeopardy of your nation. The consequences would be just the opposite and would surely lead to greater security. In connection with the reunification of Germany, the United States is prepared, along with others, to negotiate specific arrangements regarding force levels and deployments, and broad treaty undertakings, not merely against aggression but assuring positive reaction should aggression occur in Europe.

The second situation to which I refer is that of the countries of Eastern Europe. The Heads of our two Governments, together with the Prime Minister of the United Kingdom, agreed in 1945 that the peoples of these countries should have the right to choose the form of government under which they would live, and that our three countries had a responsibility in this respect. The three of us agreed to foster the conditions under which these peoples could exercise their right of free choice.

That agreement has not as yet been fulfilled.

I know that your government is reluctant to discuss these matters or to treat them as a matter of international concern. But the Heads of Governments did agree at Yalta in 1945 that these matters *were* of international concern and we specifically agreed that there could appropriately be international consultation with reference to them.

This was another matter taken up at our meeting in Geneva in 1955. You then took the position that there were no grounds for discussing this question at our confidence and that it would involve interference in the internal affairs of the Eastern European states.

But have not subsequent developments shown that I was justified in my appeal to you for consideration of these matters? Surely the Hungarian developments and the virtually unanimous action of the United Nations General Assembly in relation thereto show that conditions in Eastern Europe are regarded throughout the world as much more than a matter of purely domestic scope.

I propose that we should now discuss this matter. There is an intrinsic need of this in the interest of peace and justice, which seems to me compelling.

(3) I now make, Mr. Chairman, a proposal to solve what I consider to be the most important problem which faces the world today.

(a) I propose that we agree that outer space should be used only for peaceful purposes. We face a decisive moment in history in relation to this matter. Both the Soviet Union and the United States are now using outer space for the testing of missiles designed for military purposes. The time to stop is now.

I recall to you that a decade ago, when the United States had a monopoly of atomic weapons and of atomic experience, we offered to renounce the making of atomic weapons and to make the use of atomic energy an international asset for peaceful purposes only. If only that offer had been accepted by the Soviet Union, there would not now be the danger from nuclear weapons which you describe.

The nations of the world face today another choice perhaps even more momentous than that of 1948. That relates to the use of outer space. Let us this time, and in time, make the right choice, the peaceful choice.

There are about to be perfected and produced powerful new weapons which, availing of outer space, will greatly increase the capacity of the human race to destroy itself. If indeed it be the view of the Soviet Union that we should not go on producing ever newer types of weapons, can we not stop the production of such weapons which would use or, more accurately, misuse, outer space, now for the first time opening up as a field for man's exploration? Should not outer space be dedicated to the peaceful uses of mankind and denied to the purposes of war? That is my proposal.

(b) Let us also end the now unrestrained production of nuclear weapons. This too would be responsive to your urging against "the production of ever newer types of weapons." It is possible to assure that newly produced fissionable material should not be used for weapons purposes. Also existing weapons stocks can be steadily reduced by ascertainable transfers to peaceful purposes. Since our existing weapons stocks are doubtless larger than yours we would expect to make a greater transfer than you to peaceful purposes stocks. I should be glad to receive your suggestion as to what you consider to be an equitable ratio in this respect.

(c) I propose that, as part of such a program which will reliably check and reverse the accumulation of nuclear weapons, we stop the testing of nuclear weapons, not just for two or three years, but indefinitely. So long as the accumulation of these weapons continues unchecked, it is better that we should be able to devise weapons which will be primarily significant from a military and defensive standpoint and progressively eliminate weapons which could destroy, through fall-out, vast segments of human life. But if the production is to be stopped and the trend reversed, as I propose, then testing is no longer so necessary.

(d) Let us at the same time take steps to begin the controlled and progressive reduction of conventional weapons and military manpower.

(e) I also renew my proposal that we begin progressively to take measures to guarantee against the possibility of surprise attack. I recall, Mr. Chairman, that we began to discuss this at our personal meeting two and a half years ago, but nothing has happened although there is open a wide range of choices as to where to begin.

The capacity to verify the fulfillment of commitments is of the essence in all these matters, including the reduction of conventional forces and weapons, and it would surely be useful for us to study together through technical groups what are the possibilities in this respect upon which we could build if we then decide to do so. These technical studies could, if you wish, be undertaken without commitment as to ultimate acceptance, or as to the interdependence, of the propositions involved. It is such technical studies of the possibilities of verification and supervision that the United Nations has proposed as a first step. I believe that this is a first step that would promote hope in both of our countries and in the world. Therefore I urge that this first step be undertaken.

I have noted your conclusion, Mr. Chairman, that you attach great importance to personal contact between statesmen and that you for your part would be prepared to come to an agreement on a personal meeting of state leaders to discuss both the problems mentioned in your letter and other problems.

I too believe that such personal contacts can be of value. I showed that by coming to Geneva in the summer of 1955. I have repeatedly stated that there is nothing I would not do to advance the cause of a just and durable peace.

But meetings between us do not automatically produce good results. Preparatory work, with good will on both sides, is a prerequisite to success. High level meetings, in which we both participate, create great expectations and for that reason involve a danger of disillusionment, dejection and increased distrust if in fact the meetings are ill-prepared, if they evade the root causes of danger, if they are used primarily for propaganda, or if agreements arrived at are not fulfilled.

Consequently, Mr. Chairman, this is my proposal:

I am ready to meet with the Soviet leaders to discuss the proposals mentioned in your letter and the proposals which I make, with the attendance as appropriate of leaders of other states which have recognized responsibilities in relation to one or another of the subjects we are to discuss. It would be essential that prior to such a meeting these complex matters should be worked on in advance through diplomatic channels and by our Foreign Ministers, so that the issues can be presented in form suitable for our decisions and so that it can be ascertained that such a top-level meeting would, in fact, hold good hope of advancing the cause of peace and justice in the world. Arrangements should also be made for the appropriate inclusion, in the preparatory work, of other governments to which I allude.

I have made proposals which seem to me to be worthy of our attention and which correspond to the gravity of our times. They deal with the basic problems which press upon us and which if unresolved would make it ever more difficult to maintain the peace. The Soviet leaders by giving evidence of a genuine intention to resolve these basic problems can make an indispensable contribution to clearing away the obstacles to those friendly relations and peaceful pursuits which the peoples of all the world demand.

Sincerely,

DWIGHT D. EISENHOWER

SPECIAL MESSAGE TO THE CONGRESS
● SPACE SCIENCE AND EXPLORATION
April 2, 1958

*In this message the President discussed the report of his Science
Advisory Committee in regard to outer space, indicating man's
desire to explore the unknown; the need to take full advantage of
the military potential of space, the effects on national prestige; and
the opportunities for scientific advancement. In order to coordinate
all efforts the President asked Congress to create the National
Aeronautics and Space Agency with the necessary powers to push
forward America's space efforts.*

To the Congress of the United States:

Recent developments in long-range rockets for military purposes have for
the first time provided man with new machinery so powerful that it can put
satellites into orbit, and eventually provide the means for space exploration.
The United States of America and the Union of Soviet Socialist Republics
have already successfully placed in orbit a number of earth satellites. In
fact, it is now within the means of any technologically advanced nation to
embark upon practicable programs for exploring outer space. The early
enactment of appropriate legislation will help assure that the United States
takes full advantage of the knowledge of its scientists, the skill of its
engineers and technicians, and the resourcefulness of its industry in meeting
the challenges of the space age.

During the past several months my Special Assistant for Science and
Technology and the President's Science Advisory Committee, of which he is
the Chairman, have been conducting a study of the purposes to be served by a
national space program, of the types of projects which will be involved, and of
the problems of organizing for space science functions. In a statement which
I released on March 26, 1958, the Science Advisory Committee has listed four
factors which in its judgment give urgency and inevitability to advancement
in space technology. These factors are: (1) the compelling urge of man to
explore the unknown; (2) the need to assure that full advantage is taken of the
military potential of space; (3) the effect on national prestige of accomplishment in space science and exploration; and (4) the opportunities for
scientific observation and experimentation which will add to our knowledge
of the earth, the solar system, and the universe.

These factors have such a direct bearing on the future progress as well as on
the security of our Nation that an imaginative and well-conceived space
program must be given high priority and a sound organization provided to
carry it out. Such a program and the organization which I recommend should
contribute to (1) the expansion of human knowledge of outer space and the

use of space technology for scientific inquiry, (2) the improvement of the usefulness and efficiency of aircraft, (3) the development of vehicles capable of carrying instruments, equipment and living organisms into space, (4) the preservation of the role of the United States as a leader in aeronautical and space science and technology, (5) the making available of discoveries of military value to agencies directly concerned with national security, (6) the promotion of cooperation with other nations in space science and technology, and (7) assuring the most effective utilization of the scientific and engineering resources of the United States and the avoidance of duplication of facilities and equipment.

I recommend that aeronautical and space science activities sponsored by the United States be conducted under the direction of a civilian agency, except for those projects primarily associated with military requirements. . . . A civilian setting for the administration of space function will emphasize the concern of our Nation that outer space be devoted to peaceful and scientific purposes.

I am, therefore, recommending that the responsibility for administering the civilian space science and exploration program be lodged in a new National Aeronautics and Space Agency, into which the National Advisory Committee for Aeronautics would be absorbed. . . .

In order to assist the President and the Director of the National Aeronautics and Space Agency, I recommend that a National Aeronautics and Space Board, appointed by the President, be created. Several of the members of the Board should be from the Government agencies with the most direct interest in aeronautics, space science, and space technology. To assure that military factors are considered by the Board, at least one member should be appointed from the Department of Defense. Members appointed from outside the Government should be eminent in science, engineering, technology, education or public affairs and be selected solely because they have established records of distinguished achievement.

The National Aeronautics and Space Agency should be given that authority which it will need to administer successfully the new programs under conditions that cannot now be fully foreseen.

In order that the Agency may attract and retain the services of scientists and technicians which it must have to carry out its responsibilities with full effectiveness, it should have the authority, subject to regulations prescribed by the President, to fix the compensation of its employees at rates reasonably competitive with those paid by other employers for comparable work without regard to the provisions of existing classification laws.

The Agency should have the power to conduct research projects in its own facilities or by contract with other qualified organizations. It will thus be free to enlist the skills and resources required for the space program wherever they may be found, and to do so under the arrangements most satisfactory to all concerned. Provision should also be made for continuing and further enhancing the close and effective cooperation with the military departments which has characterized the work of the National Advisory Committee for Aeronautics. Under such cooperative arrangements it is expected that the National Aeronautics and Space Agency will perform research required in the furtherance of strictly military aeronautics and space objectives, just as the National Advisory Committee for Aeronautics now carries on important research work for the military services in aerodynamics, propulsion, materials and other fields important to the development of military aircraft and missiles.

The National Advisory Committee for Aeronautics is already engaged in research directly related to flight outside the earth's atmosphere and has research facilities adapted to work in space science. Upon the enactment of legislation carrying out my recommendations, all of the resources of the National Advisory Committee for Aeronautics would immediately come under the direction of the new Agency. . . .

Pending enactment of legislation, it is essential that necessary work relating to space programs be continued without loss of momentum. For this reason, I have approved, as part of an interim program of space technology and exploration, the launching of a number of unmanned space vehicles under the direction of the Advanced Research Projects Agency of the Department of Defense. The projects which I have approved include both scientific earth satellites and programs to explore space. . . .

I am requesting the Department of Defense and the National Advisory Committee for Aeronautics to review pertinent programs of the Department and to recommend to me those which should be placed under the direction of the new Agency. I have also asked that they prepare an operating plan to assure support of the new Agency by organizations, facilities, and other resources of the Department of Defense, either by cooperative arrangements or by transfer to the new Agency.

It is contemplated that the Department of Defense will continue to be responsible for space activities peculiar to or primarily associated with military weapons systems or military operations. Responsibility for other programs is to be assumed by the new Agency. . . .

SPECIAL MESSAGE TO CONGRESS
CIVIL RIGHTS
February 5, 1959

Two basic principles of our government are the supremacy of the law and equal protection of the laws for everyone regardless of race, religion, or national origins. In order to guarantee these principles President Eisenhower recommended several measures be enacted by Congress first to strengthen the law so that obstruction of Court orders in school desegregation cases are a Federal offense; second giving additional investigatory powers to the Federal Bureau of Investigation in case of attacks upon schools or churches. Third, the Attorney-General be given power to inspect Federal election results so as to help guarantee the right to vote; fourth, temporary financial and technical aid to assist in school desegregation; fifth, temporary provision when public schools have been closed because of desegregation decisions or orders; and sixth, that Congress consider establishing a Commission on Equal Job Opportunity under Government Contracts; and 7th extension of the Civil Rights Commission for an additional two years.

To the Congress of the United States:

Two principles basic to our system of government are that the rule of law is supreme, and that every individual regardless of his race, religion, or national origin is entitled to the equal protection of the laws. We must continue to seek every practicable means for reinforcing these principles and making them a reality for all.

The United States has a vital stake in striving wisely to achieve the goal of full equality under law for all people. On several occasions I have stated that progress toward this goal depends not on laws alone but on building a better understanding. It is thus important to remember that any further legislation in this field must be clearly designed to continue the substantial progress that has taken place in the past few years. The recommendations for legislation which I am making have been weighed and formulated with this in mind.

First, I recommend legislation to strengthen the law dealing with obstructions of justice so as to provide expressly that the use of force or threats of force to obstruct Court orders in school desegregation cases shall be a Federal offense.

There have been instances where extremists have attempted by mob violence and other concerted threats of violence to obstruct the accomplishment of the objectives in school decrees. There is a serious question whether the present obstruction of justice statute reaches such acts of obstruction which occur after the completion of the court proceedings. Nor is the contempt power a satisfactory enforcement weapon to deal with persons who seek to obstruct court decrees by such means.

The legislation that I am recommending would correct a deficiency in the present law and would be a valuable enforcement power on which the government could rely to deter mob violence and such other acts of violence or threats which seek to obstruct court decrees in desegregation cases.

Second, I recommend legislation to confer additional investigative authority on the FBI in the case of crimes involving the destruction or attempted destruction of schools or churches, by making flight from one State to another to avoid detention or prosecution for such a crime a Federal offense.

All decent, self-respecting persons deplore the recent incidents of bombings of schools and places of worship. While State authorities have been diligent in their execution of local laws dealing with these crimes, a basis for supplementary action by the federal government is needed.

Such recommendation when enacted would make it clear that the FBI has full authority to assist in investigations of crimes involving bombings of schools and churches. At the same time, the legislation would preserve the primary responsibility for law enforcement in local law enforcement agencies for crimes committed against local property.

Third, I recommend legislation to give the Attorney General power to inspect Federal election records, and to require that such records be preserved for a reasonable period of time so as to permit such inspection.

The right to vote, the keystone of democratic self-government, must be available to all qualified citizens without discrimination. Until the enactment of the Civil Rights Act of 1957, the government could protect this right only through criminal prosecutions instituted after the right had been infringed. The 1957 Act attempted to remedy this deficiency by authorizing the Attorney General to institute civil proceedings to prevent such infringements before they occurred.

A serious obstacle has developed which minimizes the effectiveness of this legislation. Access to registration records is essential to determine whether the denial of the franchise was in furtherance of a pattern of racial discrimination. But during preliminary investigations of complaints the Department of Justice, unlike the Civil Rights Commission, has no authority to require the production of election records in a civil proceeding. State or local authorities, in some instances, have refused to permit the inspection of their election records in the course of investigations. Supplemental legislation, therefore, is needed.

Fourth, I recommend legislation to provide a temporary program of financial and technical aid to State and local agencies to assist them in making the necessary adjustments required by school desegregation decisions.

The Department of Health, Education, and Welfare should be authorized to assist and cooperate with those States which have previously required or permitted racially segregated public schools, and which must now develop programs of desegregation. Such assistance should consist of sharing the burdens of transition through grants-in-aid to help meet additional costs directly occasioned by desegregation programs, and also of making technical information and assistance available to State and local educational agencies in preparing and implementing desegregation programs.

I also recommend that the Commissioner of Education be specifically authorized, at the request of the States or local agencies, to provide technical assistance in the development of desegregation programs and to initiate or participate in conferences called to help resolve educational problems arising as a result of efforts to desegregate.

Fifth, I recommend legislation to authorize, on a temporary basis, provision for the education of children of members of the Armed Forces when State-administered public schools have been closed because of desegregation decisions or orders.

The Federal Government has a particular responsibility for the children of military personnel in Federally affected areas, since Armed Services personnel are located there under military orders rather than of their own free choice. Under the present law, the Commissioner of Education may provide for the eduction of children of military personnel only in the case of those who live on military reservations or other Federal property. The legislation I am recommending would remove this limitation.

Sixth, I recommend that Congress give consideration to the establishing of a statutory Commission on Equal Job Opportunity under Government Contracts.

Non-discrimination in employment under government contracts is required by Executive Orders. Through education, mediation, and persuasion, the existing Committee on Government Contracts has sought to give effect not only to this contractual obligation, but to the policy of equal job opportunities generally. While the program has been widely accepted by government agencies, employers and unions, and significant progress has been made, full implementation of the policy would be materially advanced by the creation of a statutory Commission.

Seventh, I recommend legislation to extend the life of the Civil Rights Commission for an additional two years. While the Commission should make an interim report this year within the time originally fixed by law for the making of its final report, because of the delay in getting the Commission appointed and staffed, an additional two years should be provided for the completion of its task and the making of its final report.

I urge the prompt consideration of these seven proposals.

RADIO AND TELEVISION REPORT
TO THE AMERICAN PEOPLE
THE EVENTS IN PARIS
May 25, 1960

*President Eisenhower stated that during the past year negotiations
had been conducted which seemed to indicate a willingness on the
part of the Soviet Union to discuss some of the most pressing
problems: disarmament, mutual inspection, atomic control, and
Germany including Berlin. The United States still had to maintain
all security arrangements including the U-2 flights. Chairman
Khrushchev maintained that he knew about such flights when he had
visited the United States in September, 1959, but he never made an
issue of them until Paris. Secrecy had surrounded the first
statements of the Government because it did not know of the actual
condition of the pilot. Khrushchev demanded of the United States a
full apology, punishment of those responsible for the flight, and
assurance that they would no longer be flown. President Eisenhower
insisted that although the Russians were not reasonable the United
States must maintain businesslike relations with the Soviets and at
the same time maintain its strength and prestige. His offer to permit
Soviet reconaissance over the United States on a reciprocal basis
with Russia is still open. The United Nations might in fact take over
this task. The major aim of the United States is to foster freedom.*

My fellow Americans:

Tonight I want to talk with you about the remarkable events last week in
Paris, and their meaning to our future. . . .

You recall, of course, why I went to Paris ten days ago.

Last summer and fall I had many conversations with world leaders; some of
these were with Chairman Khrushchev, here in America. Over those months a
small improvement in relations between the Soviet Union and the West
seemed discernible. A possibility developed that the Soviet leaders might at
last be ready for serious talks about our most persistent problems—those of
disarmament, mutual inspection, atomic control, and Germany, including
Berlin.

To explore that possibility, our own and the British and French leaders met
together, and later we agreed, with the Soviet leaders, to gather in Paris on
May 16.

Of course we had no indication or thought that basic Soviet policies had
turned about. But when there is even the slightest chance of strengthening
peace, there can be no higher obligation than to pursue it.

Nor had our own policies changed. We did hope to make some progress in a Summit meeting, unpromising though previous experiences had been. But as we made preparations for this meeting, we did not drop our guard nor relax our vigilance.

Our safety, and that of the free world, demand, of course, effective systems for gathering information about the military capabilities of other powerful nations, especially those that make a fetish of secrecy. This involves many techniques and methods. In these times of vast military machines and nuclear-tipped missiles, the ferreting out of this information is indispensable to free world security.

This has long been one of my most serious preoccupations. It is part of my grave responsibility, within the overall problem of protecting the American people, to guard ourselves and our allies against surprise attack.

During the period leading up to World War II we learned from bitter experience the imperative necessity of a continuous gathering of intelligence information, the maintenance of military communications and contact, and alertness of command. . . .

Moreover, as President, charged by the Constitution with the conduct of America's foreign relations, and as Commander-in-Chief, charged with the direction of the operations and activities of our Armed Forces and their supporting services, I take full responsibility for approving all the various programs undertaken by our government to secure and evaluate military intelligence.

It was in the prosecution of one of these intelligence programs that the widely publicized U-2 incident occurred.

Aerial photography has been one of many methods we have used to keep ourselves and the free world abreast of major Soviet military developments. The usefulness of this work has been well established through four years of effort. The Soviets were well aware of it. Chairman Khrushchev has stated that he became aware of these flights several years ago. Only last week, in his Paris press conference, Chairman Khrushchev confirmed that he knew of these flights when he visited the United States last September.

Incidentally, this raises the natural question—why all the furor concerning one particular flight? He did not, when in America last September charge that these flights were any threat to Soviet safety. He did not then see any reason to confer with American representatives.

This he did only about the flight that unfortunately failed, on May 1, far inside Russia.

Now, two questions have been raised about this particular flight; first, as to its timing, considering the imminence of the Summit meeting; second, our initial statements when we learned the flight had failed.

As to the timing, the question was really whether to halt the program and thus forego the gathering of important information that was essential and that was likely to be unvavilable at a later date. The decision was that the program should not be halted.

The plain truth is this: when a nation needs intelligence activity, there is no time when vigilance can be relaxed. Incidentally, from Pearl Harbor we learned that even negotiation itself can be used to conceal preparations for a surprise attack.

Next, as to our government's initial statement about the flight, this was issued to protect the pilot, his mission, and our intelligence processes, at a time when the true facts were still undetermined.

Our first information about the failure of this mission did not disclose whether the pilot was still alive, was trying to escape, was avoiding interrogation, or whether both plane and pilot had been destroyed. Protection of our intelligence system and the pilot, and concealment of the plane's mission, seemed imperative. It must be remembered that over a long period, these flights had given us information of the greatest importance to the nation's security. In fact, their success has been nothing short of remarkable.

For these reasons, what is known in intelligence circles as a "covering statement" was issued. It was issued on assumptions that were later proved incorrect. Consequently, when later the status of the pilot was definitely established, and there was no further possibility of avoiding exposure of the project, the factual details were set forth.

I then made two facts clear to the public: first, our program of aerial reconnaissance had been undertaken with my approval; second, this government is compelled to keep abreast, by one means or another, of military activities of the Soviets, just as their government has for years engaged in espionage activities in our country and throughout the world. Our necessity to proceed with such activities was also asserted by our Secretary of State who, however, had been careful—as was I—not to say that these particular flights would be continued.

In fact, before leaving Washington, I had directed that these U-2 flights be stopped. Clearly their usefulness was impaired. . . .

Now I wanted no public announcement of this decision until I could personally disclose it at the Summit meeting in conjunction with certain proposals I had prepared for the conference.

At my first Paris meeting with Mr. Khrushchev, and before his tirade was made public, I informed him of this discontinuance and the character of the constructive proposals I planned to make. These contemplated the establishment of a system of aerial surveillance operated by the United Nations.

The day before the first scheduled meeting, Mr. Khrushchev had advised President de Gaulle and Prime Minister Macmillan that he would make certain demands upon the United States as a precondition for beginning a Summit conference.

Although the United States was the only power against which he expressed his displeasure, he did not communicate this information to me. I was, of course, informed by our allies.

At the four-power meeting on Monday morning, he demanded of the United States four things: first, condemnation of U-2 flights as a method of espionage; second, assurance that they would not be continued; third, a public apology on behalf of the United States; and, fourth, punishment of all those who had any responsibility respecting this particular mission.

I replied by advising the Soviet leader that I had, during the previous week, stopped these flights and that they would not be resumed. I offered also to discuss the matter with him in personal meetings, while the regular business of the Summit might proceed. Obviously, I would not respond to his extreme demands. He knew, of course, by holding to those demands the Soviet Union was scuttling the Summit Conference.

In torpedoing the conference, Mr. Khrushchev claimed that he acted as the result of his own moral indignation over alleged American acts of aggression. He had known of these flights for a long time. It is apparent that the Soviets had decided even before the Soviet delegation left Moscow that my trip to the Soviet Union should be cancelled and that nothing constructive from their viewpoint would come out of the Summit Conference.

In evaluating the results, however, I think we must not write the record all in red ink. There are several things to be written in the black. Perhaps the Soviet action has turned the clock back in some measure, but it should be noted that Mr. Khrushchev did not go beyond invective—a time-worn Soviet device to achieve an immediate objective. In this case, the wrecking of the Conference.

On our side, at Paris, we demonstrated once again America's willingness, and that of her allies, always to go the extra mile in behalf of peace. Once again, Soviet intransigence reminded us all of the unpredictability of despotic rule, and the need for those who work for freedom to stand together in determination and in strength.

The conduct of our allies was magnificent. My colleagues and friends— President de Gaulle and Prime Minister Macmillan—stood sturdily with the American delegation in spite of persistent Soviet attempts to split the Western group. The NATO meeting after the Paris Conference showed unprecedented unity and support for the alliance and for the position taken at the Summit meeting. I salute our allies for us all.

And now, most importantly, what about the future?

All of us know that, whether started deliberately or accidentally, global war would leave civilization in a shambles. This is as true of the Soviet system as of all others. In a nuclear war there can be no victors—only losers. Even despots understand this. Mr. Khrushchev stated last week that he well realizes that general nuclear war would bring catastrophe for both sides. Recognition of this mutual destructive capability is the basic reality of our present relations. Most assuredly, however, this does not meant that we shall ever give up trying to build a more sane and hopeful reality—a better foundation for our common relations.

To do this, here are the policies we must follow, and to these I am confident the great majority of our people, regardless of party, give their support:

First. We must keep up our strength, and hold it steady for the long pull—a strength not neglected in complacency nor overbuilt in hysteria. So doing, we can make it clear to everyone that there can be no gain in the use of pressure tactics or aggression against us and our Allies.

Second. We must continue businesslike dealings with the Soviet leaders on outstanding issues, and improve the contacts between our own and the Soviet peoples, making clear that the path of reason and common sense is still open if the Soviets will but use it.

Third. To improve world conditions in which human freedom can flourish, we must continue to move ahead with positive programs at home and abroad, in collaboration with free nations everywhere. In doing so, we shall continue to give our strong support to the United Nations and the great principles for which it stands.

Now as to the first of these purposes—our defenses are sound. They are tailored to the situation confronting us.

Their adequacy has been my primary concern for these past seven years—indeed throughout my adult life.

In no respect have the composition and size of our forces been based on or affected by any Soviet blandishment. Nor will they be. We will continue to carry forward the great improvements already planned in these forces. They will be kept ready—and under constant review.

Any changes made necessary by technological advances or world events will be recommended at once.

This strength—by far the most potent on earth—is, I emphasize, for deterrent, defensive and retaliatory purposes only, without threat or aggressive intent toward anyone.

Concerning the second part of our policy—relations with the Soviets—we and all the world realize, despite our recent disappointment, that progress toward the goal of mutual understanding, easing the causes of tensions, and reduction of armaments is as necessary as ever.

We shall continue these peaceful efforts, including participation in the existing negotiations with the Soviet Union. In these negotiations we have made some progress. We are prepared to preserve and build on it. The Allied Paris communique and my own statement on returning to the United States should have made this abundantly clear to the Soviet government.

We conduct these negotiations not on the basis of surface harmony nor are we deterred by any bad deportment we meet. Rather we approach them as a careful search for common interests between the Western allies and the Soviet Union on specific problems.

I have in mind, particularly, the nuclear test and disarmament negotiations. We shall not back away, on account of recent events, from the efforts or commitments that we have undertaken.

Nor shall we relax our search for new means of reducing the risk of war by miscalculation, and of achieving verifiable arms control.

A major American goal is a world of open societies.

Here in our country anyone can buy maps and aerial photographs showing our cities, our dams, our plants, our highways—indeed, our whole industrial and economic complex. We know that Soviet attaches regularly collect this information. Last fall Chairman Khrushchev's train passed no more than a few hundred feet from an operational ICBM, in plain view from his window. Our thousands of books and scientific journals, our magazines, newspapers and official publications, our radio and television, all openly describe to all the world every aspect of our society.

This is as it should be. We are proud of our freedom.

Soviet distrust, however, does still remain. To allay these misgivings I offered five years ago to open our skies to Soviet reconnaissance aircraft on a reciprocal basis. The Soviets refused. That offer is still open. At an appropriate time America will submit such a program to the United Nations, together with the recommendation that the United Nations itself conduct this reconnaissance. Should the United Nations accept this proposal, I am prepared to propose that America supply part of the aircraft and equipment required. . . .

Indeed, if the United Nations should undertake this policy, this program, and the great nations of the world should accept it, I am convinced that not only can all humanity be assured that they are safe from any surprise attack from any quarter, but indeed the greatest tensions of all, the fear of war, would be removed from the world. I sincerely hope that the United Nations may adopt such a program.

As far as we in America are concerned, our programs for increased contacts between all peoples will continue. Despite the suddenly expressed hostility of the men in the Kremlin, I remain convinced that the basic longings of the Soviet people are much like our own. I believe that Soviet citizens have a sincere friendship for the people of America. I deeply believe that above all else they want a lasting peace and a chance for a more abundant life in place of more and more instruments of war.

Finally, turning to the third part of America's policy—the strengthening of freedom—we must do far more than concern ourselves with military defense against, and our relations with, the Communist Bloc. Beyond this, we must advance constructive programs throughout the world for the betterment of peoples in the newly developing nations. The zigs and zags of the Kremlin cannot be allowed to disturb our worldwide programs and purposes. In the period ahead, these programs could well be the decisive factor in our persistent search for peace in freedom.

To the peoples in the newly developing nations urgently needed help will surely come. If it does not come from us and our friends, these peoples will be driven to seek it from the enemies of freedom. Moreover, those joined with us in defense partnerships look to us for proof of our steadfastness. We must not relax our common security efforts.

As to this, there is something specific all of us can do, and right now. It is imperative that crippling cuts not be made in the appropriations recommended for Mutual Security, whether economic or military. We must support this program with all of our wisdom and all of our strength. We are proud to call this a nation of the people. With the people knowing the importance of this program, and making their voices heard in its behalf throughout the land, there can be no doubt of its continued success. . . .

Thank you, and good night.

FAREWELL RADIO AND TELEVISION ADDRESS TO THE AMERICAN PEOPLE
January 17, 1961

President Eisenhower discussed his relationship with Congress; America's position in the world; America's attempts to create a peaceful world; the development of the armed forces of the United States which is related to maintaining a peaceful atmosphere; and the attempts to make agreements concerning disarmament. He warned of the potential danger of a military-industrial complex.

My fellow Americans:

Three days from now, after half a century in the service of our country, I shall lay down the responsibilities of office as, in traditional and solemn ceremony, the authority of the Presidency is vested in my successor.

This evening I come to you with a message of leave-taking and farewell, and to share a few final thoughts with you, my countrymen.

Like every other citizen, I wish the new President, and all who will labor with him, Godspeed. I pray that the coming years will be blessed with peace and prosperity for all.

Our people expect their President and the Congress to find essential agreement on issues of great moment, the wise resolution of which will better shape the future of the Nation.

My own relations with the Congress, which began on a remote and tenuous basis when, long ago, a member of the Senate appointed me to West Point, have since ranged to the intimate during the war and immediate post-war period, and, finally, to the mutually interdependent during these past eight years.

In this final relationship, the Congress and the Administration have, on most vital issues, cooperated well, to serve the national good rather than mere partisanship, and so have assured that the business of the Nation should go forward. So, my official relationship with the Congress ends in a feeling, on my part, of gratitude that we have been able to do so much together.

We now stand ten years past the midpoint of a century that has witnessed four major wars among great nations. Three of these involved our own country. Despite these holocausts America is today the strongest, the most influential and most productive nation in the world. Understandably proud of this pre-eminence, we yet realize that America's leadership and prestige depend, not merely upon our unmatched material progress, riches and military strength, but on how we use our power in the interests of world peace and human betterment.

Throughout America's adventure in free government, our basic purposes have been to keep the peace; to foster progress in human achievement, and to enhance liberty, dignity and integrity among people and among nations. To strive for less would be unworthy of a free and religious people. Any failure traceable to arrogance, or our lack of comprehension or readiness to sacrifice would inflict upon us grievous hurt both at home and abroad.

Progress toward these noble goals is persistently threatened by the conflict now engulfing the world. It commands our whole attention, absorbs our very beings. We face a hostile ideology—global in scope, atheistic in character, ruthless in purpose, and insidious in method. Unhappily the danger it poses promises to be of indefinite duration. To meet it successfully, there is called for, not so much the emotional and transitory sacrifices of crisis, but rather those which enable us to carry forward steadily, surely, and without complaint the burdens of a prolonged and complex struggle—with liberty the stake. Only thus shall we remain, despite every provocation, on our charted course toward permanent peace and human betterment.

Crises there will continue to be. In meeting them, whether foreign or domestic, great or small, there is a recurring temptation to feel that some spectacular and costly action could become the miraculous solution to all current difficulties. A huge increase in newer elements of our defense; development of unrealistic programs to cure every ill in agriculture; a dramatic expansion in basic and applied research—these and many other possibilities, each possibly promising in itself, may be suggested as the only way to the road we wish to travel.

But each proposal must be weighed in the light of a broader consideration: the need to maintain balance in and among national programs—balance between the private and the public economy, balance between cost and hoped for advantage—balance between the clearly necessary and the comfortably desirable; balance between our essential requirements as a nation and the duties imposed by the nation upon the individual; balance between actions of the moment and the national welfare of the future. Good judgment seeks balance and progress; lack of it eventually finds imbalance and frustration.

The record of many decades stands as proof that our people and their government have, in the main, understood these truths and have responded to them well, in the face of stress and threat. But threats, new in kind or degree, constantly arise. I mention two only.

A vital element in keeping the peace is our military establishment. Our arms must be mighty, ready for instant action, so that no potential aggressor may be tempted to risk his own destruction.

Our military organization today bears little relation to that known by any of my predecessors in peacetime, or indeed by the fighting men of World War II or Korea.

Until the latest of our world conflicts, the United States had no armaments industry. American makers of plowshares could, with time and as required, make swords as well. But now we can no longer risk emergency improvisation of national defense; we have been compelled to create a permanent armaments industry of vast proportions. Added to this, three and a half million men and women are directly engaged in the defense establishment. We annually spend on military security more than the net income of all United States corporations.

This conjunction of an immense military establishment and a large arms industry is new in the American experience. The total influence—economic, political, even spiritual—is felt in every city, every State house, every office of the Federal government. We recognize the imperative need for this development. Yet we must not fail to comprehend its grave implications. Our toil, resources and livelihood are all involved; so is the very structure of our society.

In the councils of government, we must guard against the acquisition of unwarranted influence, whether sought or unsought, by the military-industrial complex. The potential for the disastrous rise of misplaced power exists and will persist.

We must never let the weight of this combination endanger our liberties or democratic processes. We should take nothing for granted. Only an alert and knowledgeable citizenry can compel the proper meshing of the huge industrial and military machinery of defense with our peaceful methods and goals, so that security and liberty may prosper together.

Akin to, and largely responsible for the sweeping changes in our industrial-military posture, has been the technological revolution during recent decades.

In this revolution, research has become central; it also becomes more formalized, complex, and costly. A steadily increasing share is conducted for, by, or at the direction of, the Federal government.

Today, the solitary inventor, tinkering in his shop, has been overshadowed by task forces of scientists in laboratories and testing fields. In the same fashion, the free university, historically the fountainhead of free ideas and scientific discovery, has experienced a revolution in the conduct of research. Partly because of the huge costs involved, a government contract becomes virtually a substitute for intellectual curiosity. For every old blackboard there are now hundreds of new electronic computers.

The prospect of domination of the nation's scholars by Federal employment, project allocations, and the power of money is ever present—and is gravely to be regarded.

Yet, in holding scientific research and discovery in respect, as we should, we must also be alert to the equal and opposite danger that public policy could itself become the captive of a scientific-technological elite.

It is the task of statesmanship to mold, to balance, and to integrate these and other forces, new and old, within the principles of our democratic system—ever aiming toward the supreme goals of our free society.

Another factor in maintaining balance involves the element of time. As we peer into society's future, we—you and I, and our government—must avoid the impulse to live only for today, plundering, for our own ease and convenience, the precious resources of tomorrow. We cannot mortgage the material assets of our grandchildren without risking the loss also of their political and spiritual heritage. We want democracy to survive for all generations to come, not to become the insolvent phantom of tomorrow.

Down the long lane of the history yet to be written America knows that this world of ours, ever growing smaller, must avoid becoming a community of dreadful fear and hate, and be, instead, a proud confederation of mutual trust and respect.

Such a confederation must be one of equals. The weakest must come to the conference table with the same confidence as do we, protected as we are by our moral, economic, and military strength. That table, though scarred by many past frustrations, cannot be abandoned for the certain agony of the battlefield.

Disarmament, with mutual honor and confidence, is a continuing imperative. Together we must learn how to compose differences, not with arms, but with intellect and decent purpose. Because this need is so sharp and apparent I confess that I lay down my official responsibilities in this field with a definite sense of disappointment. As one who has witnessed the horror and the lingering sadness of war—as one who knows that another war could utterly destroy this civilization which has been so slowly and painfully built over thousands of years—I wish I could say tonight that a lasting peace is in sight.

Happily, I can say that war has been avoided. Steady progress toward our ultimate goal has been made. But, so much remains to be done. As a private citizen, I shall never cease to do what little I can to help the world advance along that road.

So—in this my last good night to you as your President—I thank you for the many opportunities you have given me for public service in war and peace. I trust that in that service you find things worthy; as for the rest of it, I know you will find ways to improve performance in the future.

You and I—my fellow citizens—need to be strong in our faith that all nations, under God, will reach the goal of peace with justice. May we be ever unswerving in devotion to principle, confident but humble with power, diligent in pursuit of the Nation's great goals.

To all the peoples of the world, I once more give expression to America's prayerful and continuing aspiration:

We pray that peoples of all faiths, all races, all nations, may have their great human needs satisfied; that those now denied opportunity shall come to enjoy it to the full; that all who yearn for freedom may experience its spiritual blessings; that those who have freedom will understand, also, its heavy responsibilities; that all who are insensitive to the needs of others will learn charity; that the scourges of poverty, disease and ignorance will be made to disappear from the earth, and that, in the goodness of time, all peoples will come to live together in a peace guaranteed by the binding force of mutual respect and love.

BIBLIOGRAPHICAL AIDS

The emphasis in this and subsequent volumes in the **Presidential Chronologies** will be on the administrations of the presidents. The more important works on other aspects of their lives, either before or after their terms in office, are included since they may contribute to an understanding of the presidential careers.

The following bibliography is critically selected. Additional titles may be found in the biographies listed below and in the standard guide. The student might also wish to consult **Reader's Guide to Periodical Literature** and **Social Sciences and Humanities Index** (formerly **International Index**) for recent articles in scholarly journals.

Additional chronological information not included in this volume because it did not relate to the president may be found in the **Encyclopedia of American History**, edited by Richard B. Morris, revised edition (New York, 1965).

SOURCE MATERIALS

Public Papers of the Presidents of the United States. Dwight D. Eisenhower. 8 vols. Washington, D.C.: U.S. Government Printing Office, 1958-1961.

BIOGRAPHIES

Adams, Sherman. **Firsthand Report; the Story of the Eisenhower Administration.** New York: Harper & Row, 1961. A personal study of the Eisenhower years by the man closely associated with the President until his (Adams') banishment from Washington because of scandal. The account is colored by the author's admiration for Eisenhower.

Childs, Marquis William. **Eisenhower: Captive Hero; A Critical Study of the General and the President.** New York: Harcourt, Brace & World, 1958. An important critical study by the journalist which enables his readers to assess Eisenhower's first years in the White House.

Donovan, Robert J. **Eisenhower: The Inside Story.** New York: Harper & Row, 1956. A pro-Eisenhower biographical review of the President's first three years in office, which although it might be called campaign literature is a dispassionate and incisive analysis.

Hughes, Emmet John. **The Ordeal of Power; A Political Memoir of the Eisenhower Years.** New York: Atheneum, 1963. This former speech writer of Eisenhower indicates his disillusionment with the former President.

Larson, Arthur. **Eisenhower: The President Nobody Knew.** New York: Scribner, 1968. This work is an assessment of Eisenhower's philosophy and opinions while in the White house, applauding his handling of foreign affairs, but indicating that his management of domestic issues was somewhat ineffective.

Smith, A. Merriman. **Meet Mister Eisenhower.** New York: Harper & Row, 1955. An attempt to present an objective humanistic approach of his way of life as President.

ESSAYS

The essay on Eisenhower in the **Encyclopedia Americana** by Kevin McCann is much too brief in its analysis. Robert Lloyd Kelley's essay in the **Encyclopedia Britannica** is a good analysis of the two terms, dealing mainly with foreign affairs because of their importance. He also discusses domestic developments and problems. More detailed essays on the Presidency and Eisenhower's role in domestic as well as foreign affairs may be found in the following:

Alberg, V. "Truman and Eisenhower: Their Administrations and Campaigns," **Current History**, XLVII (October, 1964), 221-228.

Freidel, Frank. "Thirty-fourth President, 1953-1961," **National Geographic Magazine.** CXXIX (January, 1966), 90-99.

Handlin, Oscar. "Eisenhower Administration: A Self-Portrait," **Atlantic.** CCXII (November, 1963), 67-72.

Hyman, Sidney. "What is the President's True Role?" **New York Times Magazine.** September 7, 1958, 108-109.

Marshall, C.B. "Eisenhower's Second Term," **New Republic.** CLIII (November 6, 1965), 25-27.

Wimer, Kurt. "Wilson and Eisenhower: Two Experiences in Summit Diplomacy," **Contemporary Review** (1961), 284-295.

THE EISENHOWER ERA

Ambrose, Stephen E. **Eisenhower and Berlin, 1945: The Decision to Halt at the Elbe.** New York: W.W. Norton & Co., 1968. A detailed study and defense of the reasons why Eisenhower stopped before arriving at Berlin, indicating that the Allies would have had to withdraw to their previously assigned zones.

Eisenhower, Milton S. **The Wine Is Bitter; The United States and Latin America.** New York: Doubleday, 1963. Analyzing his missions to Central and South America, the President's brother discusses the role of the United States in developing the economic and political climate of these nations.

Morrow, E. Frederic. **Black Man in The White House.** New York: Coward-McCann, 1963. This diary of the first Negro to serve on a Presidential staff in an executive capacity concentrates on the author's assigned area of civil rights, indicating the reluctance of the Eisenhower administration to take bold steps on racial issues.

Smith, A. Merriman. **A President's Odyssey.** New York: Harper & Row, Publishers, 1961. A detailed analysis of the good-will tours of President Eisenhower in search of his ideal of world peace by the UPI reporter.

Smith, Walter Bedell. **Eisenhower's Six Great Decisions: Europe, 1944-1945.** New York, Longmans, Green, 1955. A review of the six major decisions made by Eisenhower during the European campaign in the Second World War by his Chief of Staff.

Snyder, Marty. **My Friend Ike.** Written with Glenn D. Kittler. New York: Fell, 1956. A warm humanistic study of Snyder's friendship with and his efforts to help in the election of Eisenhower as President. Important for the personal reminiscences, not good on politics.

WORKS BY EISENHOWER

At Ease: Stories I Tell to Friends. New York: Doubleday, 1963.
Crusade in Europe. Garden City, N.Y.: Doubleday, 1948.
Peace with Justice; Selected Addresses. New York: Popular Library, 1961.
The White House Years, vol. 1. **Mandate For Change, 1953-1956.** New York: Doubleday, 1963.
The White House Years, vol. 2. **Waging Peace, 1956-01961.** New York: Doubleday, 1965.

THE PRESIDENCY

Bailey, Thomas Andrew. **Presidential Greatness: The Image and the Man from George Washington to the Present.** New York, 1966. A good critical study of the qualities of presidential greatness, listing 43 methods for measuring presidential ability. Bailey agrees with the "Average" ranking of Eisenhower by the Schlesinger group but would put him higher than the bottom of the group.

Binkley, Wilfred E. **The Man in the White House: His Powers and His Duties.** Rev. ed. New York, 1964. A fine historically-oriented survey of the Presidency in its various aspects.

Corwin, Edward Samuel. **The President: Office and Powers; History and Analysis of Practice and Opinions.** 4th ed. New York, 1957. Although an older work, still a standard factual and well-documented historical account of the position of the President.

Kane, Joseph Nathan. **Facts about the President.** New York, 1959. Detailed factual information about each President from Washington to Eisenhower, as well as comparative data and statistics concerning the individuals and the office of the presidency.

Koenig, Louis W. **The Chief Executive.** New York, 1964. Historical discussion of presidential powers comparing America's strong and weak presidents.

Rossiter, Clinton Lawrence. **The American Presidency.** 2nd ed. New York, 1960. A fine analysis of the powers and limitations of the President.

Schlesinger, Arthur Meyer. "Our President: A Rating by 75 Historians," **New York Times Magazine**, July 29, 1962, 12 ff.

NAME INDEX

TITLES IN THE OCEANA
PRESIDENTIAL CHRONOLOGY SERIES

Reference books containing Chronology—Documents—Bibliographical Aids for each President covered.
Series Editor: **Howard F. Bremer**

GEORGE WASHINGTON*
edited by Howard F. Bremer

JOHN ADAMS*
edited by Howard F. Bremer

JAMES BUCHANAN*
edited by Irving J. Sloan

GROVER CLEVELAND**
edited by Robert I. Vexler

FRANKLIN PIERCE*
edited by Irving J. Sloan

ULYSSES S. GRANT**
edited by Philip R. Moran

MARTIN VAN BUREN**
edited by Irving J. Sloan

THEODORE ROOSEVELT**
edited by Gilbert Black

BENJAMIN HARRISON*
edited by Harry J. Sievers

JAMES MONROE*
edited by Ian Elliot

WOODROW WILSON**
edited by Robert I. Vexler

RUTHERFORD B. HAYES*
edited by Arthur Bishop

ANDREW JACKSON**
edited by Ronald Shaw

JAMES MADISON*
edited by Ian Elliot

HARRY S TRUMAN***
edited by Howard B. Furer

WARREN HARDING*
edited by Philip Moran

DWIGHT D. EISENHOWER**
edited by Robert I. Vexler

JAMES K. POLK*
edited by John J. Farrell

Available Soon

JOHN QUINCY ADAMS*
edited by Kenneth Jones

HERBERT HOOVER*
edited by Arnold Rice

ABRAHAM LINCOLN**
edited by Ian Elliot

GARFIELD/ARTHUR**
edited by Howard B. Furer

*   96 pages, $3.00/B
** 128 pages, $4.00/B
*** 160 pages, $5.00/B